PRAISE FOR *BROKEN DEALER*

Buckle up as you flip through the pages of this book, you're in for a ride alongside Daren and Carmine as they navigate the opaque world of finance, guided by a steadfast commitment to genuine service and unwavering authenticity. But be careful—once you see it, you can't unsee it.

Floyd Shilanski
Founder, Shilanski and Associates

As they say in the book, you will not meet two more different professionals who think and act as one. This is not just another book on the financial advisor world; it's THE playbook on how to break free and have it all for yourself and your family.

Joe Lukacs
Founder, Magellan Network and Mastermind

Broken Dealer stands out for its unwavering commitment to truth-telling and its emphasis on the transformative power of putting clients first. Blonski and Corino's hard-won lessons and practical advice serve as a roadmap for financial advisors ready to embark on the path of independence. This book is a must-read for anyone seeking to build a thriving, client-centered practice and is a testament to the authors' dedication to empowering others in the financial services industry.

Brian Boughner, CFA, CMT
Cofounder—The Fiduciary Alliance

BROKEN DEALER

BROKEN DEALER

NAVIGATING THE PATH TO FINANCIAL ADVISOR INDEPENDENCE

CARMINE CORINO
DAREN BLONSKI

Advantage | Books

Published by Advantage Books, Charleston, South Carolina.
An imprint of Advantage Media.

ADVANTAGE is a registered trademark, and the Advantage colophon is a trademark of Advantage Media Group, Inc.

Printed in the United States of America.

10 9 8 7 6 5 4 3 2 1

ISBN: 978-1-64225-655-0 (Paperback)
ISBN: 978-1-64225-654-3 (eBook)

Library of Congress Control Number: 2024907673

Cover design by Lance Buckley.
Layout design by Ruthie Wood.

This publication is designed to provide accurate and authoritative information in regard to the subject matter covered. It is sold with the understanding that the publisher is not engaged in rendering legal, accounting, or other professional services. If legal advice or other expert assistance is required, the services of a competent professional person should be sought.

Advantage Books is an imprint of Advantage Media Group. Advantage Media helps busy entrepreneurs, CEOs, and leaders write and publish a book to grow their business and become the authority in their field. Advantage authors comprise an exclusive community of industry professionals, idea-makers, and thought leaders. For more information go to **advantagemedia.com**.

To all those who have helped us along this journey. You know who you are.

CONTENTS

ACKNOWLEDGMENTS xi

INTRODUCTION 1
Broken Dealer

CHAPTER 1 11
Are You Prepared to Go Down This Road?

CHAPTER 2 27
Breaking Down the Business Models

CHAPTER 3 45
Start Your Own or Bolt-On?

CHAPTER 4 57
How Are You Really Getting Paid?

CHAPTER 5 71
Building Your Plan: How and When

CHAPTER 6 . . . . **93**
Messaging

CHAPTER 7 . . . . **113**
What to Expect

ABOUT THE AUTHORS **133**

ENDNOTES **135**

ACKNOWLEDGMENTS

There are many people to acknowledge for helping us tell our story in *Broken Dealer*. Many whom we could thank for their good examples, and many whom we could thank for their bad examples. But most of all, we are grateful for all of those who joined us on the journey to serve our clients.

INTRODUCTION

Broken Dealer

When one door closes, another opens; but we often look so long and so regretfully upon the closed door that we do not see the one which has opened for us.

—ALEXANDER GRAHAM BELL

Our story began when an Italian guy from Jersey and a Bay Area psychology nerd crossed paths at a financial advisors' conference in Scottsdale, Arizona. This wasn't the start of a joke but the beginning of our journey.

Seated next to each other at a Magellan Mastermind conference hosted by business coach Joe Lukacs, we found ourselves engaged in shop talk. To our surprise, we discovered an uncanny ability to finish each other's sentences and wholeheartedly agree on various topics.

Despite our different backgrounds, a striking synergy emerged. Both of us had experienced the frustration of feeling stifled and constrained within large financial firms, where profit often took precedence over client relationships. This was what we referred to as the 'golden handcuffs'—the allure of high salaries and prestige that kept us tied to these firms despite our dissatisfaction. It was clear that we shared an ethos predicated on serving clients above all else. The desire to break free from these confines and prioritize genuine service to clients became a common bond.

Unraveling the golden handcuffs and venturing away from the status quo proved to be a daunting endeavor, filled with challenges and uncertainties. Believe us, flying off from the mother ship is not for the faint of heart.

As our dialogue deepened, we realized that beneath our surface differences lay a shared foundation. While Daren pursued a career in financial advising after obtaining a master's degree in psychology, Carmine entered the profession straight out of high school. Daren's path led him through a well-known broker-dealer, while Carmine gained experience with a Fortune 500 insurance firm.

Despite our disparities, we found a common ground in our values and perspectives, a shared foundation that transcended our individual paths. We realized that we are built the same, as Carmine would say, or that we occupy the same headspace, as Daren would describe it—different words, same ideas. Many roads lead to Rome.

The notion of documenting our experiences and the valuable lessons we'd gleaned had been brewing in both our minds prior to our encounter. Now, spurred on by mutual encouragement, we've embarked on this journey together. Our shared penchant for efficiency led us to the logical conclusion: Why divide the labor of writing a book when we can collaborate seamlessly?

> Both of us had been thinking—in fact, encouraged—to
> write a book about our experiences and the lessons we
> have learned. The idea was percolating in both our minds
> before we met. Now we've taken that advice—together. We
> are both efficiency addicts, so why not divide up the work
> of writing a book?

This begins our narrative—a tale of resilience, camaraderie, and the pursuit of authenticity in the sea of sameness that is the world of financial advising.

So, Why Should You Care?

Why is it interesting that two financial advisors wrote a book about escaping two behemoth financial services firms and creating independent practices? If two guys from different backgrounds and opposite ends of the country think and feel the same about their profession, so do thousands of others. However, relatively few of them are executing the same escape plan because it takes guts to do it, not to mention fire, decisiveness, a plan, and a lot of hard work.

There are approximately 77,000 independent advisors in the United States (with no BD affiliation). We can't possibly be the only two who believe that clients should come first, that clients are better served on an independent fiduciary platform, that payout structures can create an inherent conflict of interest, that there is a process for leaving a big firm, and that relationships matter not only for business but also for a more fulfilling life. We know many colleagues who would like to make the same move but lack the knowledge and the means to do so.

We did something about it and made many surprising discoveries along the way—some painful and some inspiring. We've stepped in the potholes, stumbled over the tree roots, and learned which bear spray we should have had. (We also employ a diversified portfolio of metaphors.)

We've grown and prospered through it all, both personally and professionally. It turns out, it takes guts, but it's not a significant risk if you've cared for your clients.

Now, we offer these insights to thousands of financial advisors who know in their gut that the big transactional institutions are likely not prudently serving their customers and feel the need to shower every time they sell a product the client didn't need.

If that's your current state of mind, this book is for you. Because sharing our ethos isn't enough. How do you make the break? How do you even begin? How do you disengage from a lucrative career, leave your colleagues behind, and win your clients' trust and business all over again?

It hasn't always been easy. We faced challenges such as navigating legal and regulatory requirements, building a new client base, and managing the financial implications of the transition. It took months of soul-searching, family support, and faith in the unknown to make the break. It cost us friends and taught us whom we could rely on and couldn't. It deepened our client relationships and—maybe most importantly—helped us sleep at night. It was a complicated, painful, messy, rewarding, and ultimately inspiring process that has us both on the path to a more fulfilling career in financial services.

Oh, and as it turns out, you can also do better by doing good.

Failing to Plan Is Planning to Fail

Leaving a big firm is not for everyone. But if you're anything like us, it's the only option. If you can't sleep at night, you need a new career path. We have watched and helped many leave while learning many lessons along the way. This transition requires a focused plan and a process. You know the saying—those who fail to plan are planning to fail.

It's the mantra of our profession when applied to saving and investing. In this book, we will share what financial advisors must consider if they're thinking of breaking away, what questions they must ask themselves, and what trials and tribulations to expect. We will outline the prospects for success and how you can earn more in the long run as an independent advisor simply because you will have truthfully earned the trust of your clients. And keep in mind that while our experiences and those we communicate with others share similar aspects to your transition, your journey will be uniquely yours if you accept it.

Who are we to be pontificating on all this? Who made us these great mavens of independent financial advising? Carmine would say, "We're just a couple of Joes." Daren would say we're two ordinary financial advisors leavened by experience.

The point is, we're not unique; we're probably just like you, minus the Jersey accent, in Carmine's case. What we do have to offer, however, are the searing lessons we have learned firsthand. They say you can identify the pioneers by the arrows on their backs. Perhaps, with this book, we can spare you the wounds.

Carmine Corino, CFP®, is the founder and CEO of Cornerstone Planning Group, an independent advisory firm in New Jersey. Since 2003, he's been in the financial services industry, focused on delivering massive value to his clientele. Daren Blonski, CFP®, is the cofounder and managing principal of Fermata Advisors. He is a learner, educator, and entrepreneur. With a master's degree in psychology, he is deeply connected to helping clients take their lives to the next level.

That's what our official bios say. In reality, we're a couple of regular guys from middle-class working families with partners and kids but also with grit and determination. Our pedigree is that of "street smarts." Harvard doesn't take our type. We both worked our way up and off the ladder—Carmine at an insurance company and Daren through the brokerage environment.

Traveling the world on the big broker dime and staying at the Ritz Carlton was exhilarating for us Best Western guys. We were making great money, enjoying mind-blowing perks, building lifelong relationships, and hating ourselves for doing it.

We believed that many practices were misguided and designed to enrich the company at the client's expense. To say it plainly, we couldn't sleep at night. At every step, we felt we needed to apologize to our clients.

"When it takes thirty minutes to disclose and adequately explain your compensation structure to the client ... something is off," says Daren.

For Carmine, after years of scrapping with his employer, the final straw was a new directive to quadruple the commission generated from the products the company manufactured annually. Some clients needed life insurance, and we had decent products, so the original imperative was easily achievable without violating anyone's code of conduct. But this new approach changed everything. On a three-week safari with his family, Carmine realized he wouldn't have chosen to work for the company if he had known then what he knew now. As such, he made plans to leave.

For Daren, the epiphany occurred more quickly when his company's compliance department scolded him for referring to himself as a "financial planner." Back then, that indicated a fiduciary responsibility to the client, which they didn't want him to have. When firm compliance infrastructure tries to operate under the cloak of "suitability," having an advisor infer to the client that they are acting in the client's best interest could be considered problematic. It brought into stark relief the chasm between what Daren was working to achieve and what the company expected from him. He stuck around long enough to earn his CFP® certification, got his feet under him, and exited stage left on his own accord.

What to Expect in This Book

Throughout these chapters, we'll navigate the crucial aspects of taking the plunge, dissecting business models like insurance, broker-dealer, registered investment advisor (RIA), and hybrid setups. We'll also tackle the decision-making process between joining an existing independent firm and venturing into the wild world of starting from scratch.

We'll take you through the various ways of getting paid because sleeping at night is great, but your family needs to eat, too. With five children between us, we know firsthand the pressures of walking away from a steady paycheck. In the later chapters, we'll guide you through some of the necessary elements of a breakaway plan.

Going out on your own is an emotional roller coaster. We'll steer you for the ride. Understanding your emotions is a big part of succeeding because the movie is unexpectedly mentally challenging. That's where Daren's psychology training comes in handy. We'll prepare you emotionally and help you develop some emotional resilience.

What's in it for us? We want to share our stories and help others avoid some of the pain we endured. It would be the icing on the cake if a couple of like-minded financial advisors joined our firm, but that isn't the point. If that's your goal, writing a book is a very inefficient approach.

This book is our gift to the people in the industry we left behind, those coming up behind us, and those who haven't yet entered the business. And maybe it's a bit of catharsis after passing through a crucible our departure entailed and thriving on the other end. We are trying to positively impact our profession and hopefully, along the way, help one or many of those reading the book take the steps to independence.

So then, in the final chapter, the real journey begins. We will help you start taking the first concrete step toward independence—writing the plan. Once you have crossed the Rubicon in your mind to strike out on your own, it's time to write down the exact steps required to do it, and we'll give you the tools for that.

For us, ultimately, this book is a love story. We love our profession, work, and vision of change. We are passionate about helping our clients build wealth for a better life. We love our clients and the relationships we've built with them, and we have strong bonds with many of our industry colleagues. And maybe it's also a story of redemption and even a declaration of victory for the two of us who found a way to enjoy our careers and not feel ethically challenged.

There's a pattern, a process that if you follow, you will increase your probability of success. We, through our unique form of genius, known clinically as "dumb luck," have created that process. Having carried out the process, we know how to do it right and how to do it wrong, and we can help people who want to enjoy their lives more. Remember that this process is ever-changing; we have learned through many others and will continue to. But the items we discuss in this book should get you started.

If you agree, it's time for a self-assessment. Let's get going.

But, first, a bit of housekeeping. Two of us are writing this book together. Usually, we write in the third person because "we" are neither of us. When one of us is speaking, generally because we're telling a personal story, we will communicate in the first person.

So, unless you are reading a personal story written in the first person, you are hearing our combined story. Part of the point of this book is that we're two guys toiling away on opposite coasts with different backgrounds and yet have had parallel experiences along the way.

CHAPTER 1

ARE YOU PREPARED TO GO DOWN THIS ROAD?

A few lines of reasoning can change the way we see the world.

—STEVEN E. LANDSBURG

I was on a nineteen-day safari in Africa with my family, seeing big game not seen in North America outside zoos—elephants, hippos, lions, zebras, giraffes, warthogs, and more. It should have been magical—what dreams are made of. It was meant to be the trip of a lifetime.

(This is Carmine's story. There are thousands of stories like it in the financial advisor business, differing only in the details. Vocational epiphanies occur in many settings and in many ways, but in our corner of the forest, they all have some important commonalities. If you've had one, are in the midst of one, or are building up to one, much of this will sound familiar.)

Something was nagging at me. I'd known for years that my employer, a Fortune 500 insurance company, seemed to care more about selling products and amassing revenue than taking care of customers' needs, as if the two were mutually exclusive. I'd managed to work around their selling requirements, fend off the most egregious demands, build relationships even when the company encouraged quick transactions, and construct an impressive portfolio of clients.

My employer wanted slam-bam-thank-you-ma'am commissions. I had always turned them into how's-the-family-let's-have-coffee meetings to determine if the new product the company was pushing accrued to the client's benefit and fit into the overall plan we had developed together for them. What's important to me: I'm a people person who believes that financial planning is a collaborative process designed to provide for the long-term financial needs of my clients. This belief is more than a philosophy: it's part of my DNA, my psychological constitution. As long as clients followed me, I could stay in the firm's good graces.

In one way, the company made it effortless, frankly. They had the might of a well-capitalized corporation, economies of scale, marketplace muscle, and, consequently, reasonably priced good products. It was easy to find clients here and there who could benefit from the financial instruments they were selling, mainly when I had already earned the trust of my clients, who knew I had their best interests in mind. I could keep the corporate hounds at bay while simultaneously serving my customers.

But just before the safari, in July 2019, the dark corporate overlords decided that good enough was no longer acceptable. The massive profits, bloated Wall Street valuation, the multimillion-dollar salaries for top managers, and even the golden parachutes for C-suite mercenaries failed to slake the company's thirst for more. They quadrupled—*quadrupled*—the annual sales requirement for products that I, in good conscience, couldn't offer to four times as many clients. They simply didn't need it.

How did the company brass determine that 4× sales was the proper benchmark? Did they evaluate customer needs and link the benefits of these insurance products to determine that we had only fully served one-fifth of those who could further prosper by purchasing these products? Ha! Not likely! They looked at revenues and decided that selling proprietary products was failing to meet their goals and decided brokers could shove these products down the throats of many more customers, need be damned.

Riding in a jeep through the jungle, surrounded by these glorious creatures of the natural world, not to mention a spectacular wife and two fabulous children, I wrestled with the problem. My wife could see I wasn't fully present then, something I have always been adept at. Whether it's a kid's ball game or dinner with her, I'm good at disengaging from the mundane daily tribulations, focusing on the now, and letting my worries wait in the wings. It's more like a coping mechanism than a talent—I need to get away from the annoying gnat bites of work and concentrate on enjoying the small moments, for which I am so grateful. But on this trip, I had an elephant-sized concern diverting my attention, and my wife knew it.

It didn't take much thought to become evident that my choices were twofold: lower my ethical standards or disengage from my employer of seventeen years. I knew what staying meant, but what would leaving entail? It was a great unknown. It was a leap across a chasm without seeing the landing spot.

My Mensa Society application isn't lost in the mail. I've never been the brightest guy in the room, even alone with my kids. I'm the guy who *hires* the brightest guy in the room and lets his knowledge raise our entire team. But I can usually work out the solution to a problem, especially one involving people, their actions, and feelings. In this case, though, I needed help with what to do.

Then my wife asked me the question that brought the situation into focus: If you knew what you know now when you joined the company, would you have gone to work for them?

The answer was so obviously "no" that it immediately crystallized my decision. It was time to take the plunge.

Decisions made very quickly can be every bit as good as decisions made cautiously and deliberately.

—MALCOLM GLADWELL, BLINK

Malcolm Gladwell made the point in his best-selling book *Blink* that many of our best decisions are visceral, made in a moment based on the evidence our eyes and brains and experience can capture in a nanosecond without even passing through the processing regions of our brains. (I'm looking forward to Malcolm quoting us in his next book. It's only fair, right?)

"We live in a world that assumes that the quality of a decision is directly related to the time and effort that went into making it … We believe that we are always better off gathering as much information as possible and spending as much time as possible in deliberation. But there are moments, particularly in times of stress, when haste does not make waste, when our snap judgments and first impressions can offer a much better means of making sense of the world,"[1] he writes.

As his book demonstrates, thinking too profoundly—which sometimes means *at all*—can be the enemy of good decision-making.

Imagine that a reasonably priced Google stock drops 20 percent in one day because Elon Musk says something disparaging about it on Twitter. You don't have to puzzle out some deeper meaning to know that, as a result, you should invest chunks of money into Google.

You know almost intuitively that Google is a great company surrounded by moats against the competition, owners of their marketplace, diversified to cushion any blows to their primary service, and that Twitter is a cesspool of inanity (or worse) and also that Elon Musk is a brilliant provocateur whose ruminations should be the food for thought, perhaps, or maybe just for entertainment but not for market movement. You would be wise to execute the trades without wasting time pouring over Google's financial statements and analyzing its trailing price-to-earnings ratio (PE).

We need to respect the fact that it is possible to know without knowing why we know and accept that—sometimes—we're better off that way.

—MALCOLM GLADWELL, BLINK

It was the same for me with the decision to cut bait and fish elsewhere. I didn't just know it; I felt it in my bones. Sometimes, when the right thing to do is in front of you, you know it, even without thinking. That is the essence of *Blink* and of my decision that day in the jeep with my wife and kids while passing by the king of the jungle. So, my heart, head, and bones were all on board.

Great decision made; I just had to figure out how to execute this departure. And when. And what that meant, exactly. And who was coming with me? And that all the "I's" that needed to be dotted and "t's" that needed crossing. And a myriad of additional details, understanding that "myriad" translates to *ten thousand*. In other words, the torture I had just endured in wrestling with the decision was a mere preview of what was to come. I hadn't even reached the hard part of my journey, and, as I was to discover later, even the hard part was just the beginning because there would be even more complex parts. But let's not get ahead of ourselves.

It's Hard to Leave

The truth is most people probably don't have that "aha" moment the way Carmine did. For most of us, the realization that we are a square peg functioning in a round hole comes gradually, along with a growing awareness that we need to find our square hole. We come to understand that the larger firms prioritize the profit over the client, who is reduced to a mere transaction. But what exactly are they transacting?

We know they should ask: How is the client best served? Suppose the client has questions on budgeting; the firm views that this way: if we can't monetize that narrative with one of our advisors, then we don't want you to do it. Don't spend your time on economically unproductive exercises. But that is the job of a financial *advisor*, and besides, it's critical to success if you take a longer view and understand that we are in the relationship business.

Daren's awakening was somewhat different from Carmine's.

I came to understand the burgeoning problem, both quickly and slowly, over time. That is, I understood the fundamental disconnect from my financial services behemoth employer from the jump but took my time coming around to the circumstances to leave. There was no lightning bolt, no straw that broke the camel's back. It was a slow reckoning for me. Things were relatively good at the firm I was with. I was very successful and built a great practice with the support of other advisors in the town where I worked. However, I kept running into situations where I wanted to help a client, but the firm I was with was not very flexible.

I struggled with conundrums like this: a young executive has substantial stock options at their place of employment but minimal investible assets. Many advisors make money by taking custody of the assets at a brokerage. If the firm can't take custody of the assets, then a broker has few other options to be paid for advice. I found that some of my best work had nothing to do with managing assets but was more tied to the advice I gave centered on financial planning. So, if clients cannot move their money out of their 401(k) or stock options, there's no way to create revenue while helping them. After all, I wasn't working at a nonprofit.

Under the commission model, a financial advisor generally must find a way to generate transactions that generate fees. It's not overtly talked about but certainly always implied. Brokers and insurance agents are encouraged to sell these clients insurance policies, mutual funds, and other products loaded with invisible fees that boost the bottom line for the firm but not them. Clients then sport shiny new products that work great for the advisor and the firm that sold them without providing much value to the client and their needs. There is a better way.

Every six months, the mothership would send glossy magazines to my colleagues with photos of trips to exotic places we could take with the company if we hit our diversification requirements— a.k.a. the wide variety of products sold to clients. For a week of pampering and relaxation at the Ritz Carlton on the Caribbean Island of St. Thomas, with its white sand beaches and crystal-clear water, snorkeling, scuba diving, and margaritas, we would have to sell a certain amount of products to customers irrespective of whether they should have bought it or whether we offered the best product in its respective category.

Don't forget that on every one of these trips, I had to attend several hours of "drinking green cultural Kool-Aid" so that the firm could legitimately book it as a business expense. If advisors desired a week of pampered life, they had to manage the portfolio of employer requirements that did not necessarily correlate with client needs. Fortunately, this practice has generally been retired.

It's worth mentioning that not everyone has the same hair-on-fire desire to leave their employer but wants to, nonetheless. For a friend of Daren's who asked not to be named in our book, the problem at the big bank wasn't so much an ethical issue but one of control. He saw his colleagues get fired and escorted out for reasons he disagreed with and feared that the bank would take his book of business from him in an instant. He realized that his brokerage could "pull the rug" at any moment for any reason. After watching this, he planned his departure for months, handed in his resignation on a Friday afternoon, walked down the street to his rented office, and began making phone calls to clients—hundreds of difficult conversations over a weekend.

This friend, along with a partner, left a portfolio of one thousand clients at the bank, a completely unmanageable number that required a level of triage from the pair, leaving many—most—of their clients receiving little to no service. Think about it: a quarterly fifteen-minute conversation with each client, even if you could reach them on the first try and make arrangements for the discussion without any investment of time, would consume 250 hours or a month-and-a-half of 8-hour workdays.

Even those who work more than forty-hour weeks know that it doesn't leave enough time for the paperwork alone, much less all the other aspects of the job. The weekend after their resignations, they reached out only to the best clients. They ended up with 280 house-holds, enough to generate an excellent living while delivering much-improved service. They now schedule regular portfolio reviews, which was impossible with the sprawling spreadsheet of clients at the bank.

The incentives are turned on their head—or back on their feet—with a fiduciary model built on relationships rather than transactions. The financial advisor in a fee-based arrangement is wholly focused on the client's best interest, both because serving the client's best interest is the way to keep clients and because the more the client earns, the more the advisor earns. Making a quick "buck" isn't the focus; instead, the focus is on building long-term relationships. Motivation for both advisor and client dovetails nicely, as it should, in a fee-based model.

As our chapter heading reminds us, leaving is nonetheless difficult. It's not simply a matter of logic. Inertia being what it is, most of us remain on the job for months or years with this low-level dread gnawing at us as we grope around for the right opportunity and occasionally rally around the periodical good days on the current job. This rationale explains why the two of us know a hundred miserable financial advisors who love their field, career, and clients and tolerate their jobs but haven't yet found the key to unlocking a happier future. Change is hard; significant change is extremely hard.

Marriage counselors say marriages require about four times as many good moments as bad ones to remain viable. Marriages with more than the 4× ratio of good to bad moments demonstrate strength and long-term viability. However, those that stay consistently below three times as many good moments are bound to fail. Those between three and four times exist in purgatory; they can limp along that way for a while but generally either find some new optimistic track and get above the 4× line to remain viable or drift below 3× and end.

Still, that means most marriages that end in divorce nonetheless had many more good moments than bad (not all) about which the betrothed can rhapsodize—if only to themselves—while they remain married.

In other words, it's easy to convince yourself that things are pretty good, all things considered, after a good day, hour, or moment, especially when the alternative to feeling good about your lousy situation—a significant life change—is scary and daunting.

That's doubly true when you know that an all-expenses-paid ski trip in the Swiss Alps is within your grasp if only you endure a little more misery. That is why it's hard to leave. And that is why we've written this book. We want to replace your fear of failure, of the unknown, or the tremendous effort involved with hope for a better life for you and better results for your clients.

Once you have determined that your mental health and emotional well-being require a separation from the sales role that the corporate behemoth insists on, the next question is determining whether you are ready to cut the umbilical cord. We'll walk you through that decision and then help you determine what kind of escape you want to manufacture and how exactly to render this change. We offer you this road map not because we're brilliant theorists who have developed an innovative system that answers formerly inscrutable questions but because we're a couple of guys who crossed this raging river and got to the other side, wetter, a bit bedraggled but oh so much happier and better off for making the journey.

We can tell you where the boulders are, where the rapids are raging, what will weigh you down if you bring it along with you, what you absolutely can't leave without, and how to take each step. There is a way that happens in steps on a timeline that we know works because we've both independently taken it every step of the way ourselves.

There's a cadence to leaving a firm; if you understand the cadence and how it works, you can be very successful.

You Will Likely Make *More* Money, Not Less

This chapter brings us to a fundamental question that often holds financial advisors back from leaving the comfort and security of a big firm: Will your income take a hit? Let's face it: if you've come to the realization that the relentless pursuit of revenue by corporate financial services giants, regardless of its impact on client financial well-being, doesn't align with your client-centric values, then the primary barrier to your departure is likely compensation. Compensation, in its various forms, is a significant consideration: money, benefits, travel, perks, peace of mind, time with family, mental and emotional health, a sense of fulfillment, and so on.

The first four we've listed are monetary in one way or another, and because that is most of what the big firms have to offer, they do so in spades. The other four are nonmonetary, and if you are reading this, it's likely because you've concluded, as we did, that these elements needed to be included in your compensation portfolio. But we get it: your kids have to eat. We have five children between us, so taking a pay cut was no more on our agenda than it is on yours.

The big firm is a giant cocoon that attempts to wrap you securely and handles all your other needs while you turn the flywheel for them. They are the proverbial bird in the hand: you know what you have with them, and barring a tectonic shift in your performance or the company's reputation, you will have that every year. (It is worth noting that those tectonic shifts in the form of massive company scandals are not uncommon. Consider Wells Fargo and Lehman Brothers as two recent examples. In both cases, both complicit and innocent employees paid a steep price for the misdeeds of others, most of whom were in leadership positions.)

Taking the risk to create or join an independent, fee-based advisory firm involves stepping out on the tightrope without the safety net. Suppose you're establishing a firm of your own. In that case, it may also include going for some time without income, or at least without adding any new clients, losing some established clients, and investing in a new venture—all of which amounts to taking a risk. But who knows more about managing risk than someone who counsels clients to ride the waves of the stock market? Once you've done your due diligence about what to expect and the steps to get there, you've eliminated much of the risk and can confidently charge forward.

So, will you have a bad year financially? For instance, critical expenditures might transpire in your household—you're getting married, your spouse is returning to school, you're building an addition to your house, your mom is moving in with you, your oldest child is leaving for college, a medical emergency, etc. From our experience, the answer is likely no. You will not likely see your income decline if you follow a plan. On the contrary, for various reasons, you are more likely to see it rise the very year you depart, and don't forget the nonmonetary compensation.

First, if you follow a well-thought-out plan, you will be prepared when you do take the leap, resulting in a relatively smooth transition. Second, if you follow a plan and you've been taking care of your customers, chances are they will find you. They have a relationship with you, not necessarily with your employer. If you like your doctor and they move to another practice (that is similarly convenient and accepts your insurance), would you follow them or remain loyal to the medical practice? Almost everyone would follow the doctor they know and trust. It's the same for financial advisors, just as it is for hair stylists, dentists, insurance agents, attorneys, certified public accountants (CPAs), and others with whom we develop personal and professional relationships.

Third, following a plan will strengthen those relationships because of your honest conversations with your clients about your ability to serve their "best interests." Moving to an independent advisory firm can be a powerful engine for building a robust practice and strengthening future client relationships.

In 2020, when Carmine extricated himself from the golden handcuffs and struck out on his own, he had his best year ever—mentally, emotionally, and psychologically, but also monetarily—despite the pandemic and going five-and-a-half months without adding a single client while he laid the foundation of his new firm. How? Because of heartfelt conversations with his clients about his complete dedication to their best interests. The menu of options would no longer be limited to column A and column B from the firm; the universe of choices would now present itself to Carmine and his clients. An independent financial advisor can choose if a product "out of network" for the old employer is the best alternative for a client.

Daren and his friend who left a big bank have similar stories. Despite the drop in the stock market about halfway through his first year as principal at a fee-based, independent firm, his friend's income was higher. He attributes some of that to the better service offered to fewer clients and some to the financial independence of the new arrangement. His share of the revenue doubled from 35 percent at the bank to 70 percent now. Imagine doubling the return you could get for your clients moving from one financial instrument to another: you would do it in a New York minute, even if you live near Daren in California.

For Carmine, fattening the wallet was a multilayered operation. It wasn't one thing that boosted income; almost everything he did contributed. As a small, nimble fee-based firm, he established and leveraged an app, something the big firm, tangled up in its bureaucracy, couldn't do. With just a couple of decision-makers, Cornerstone Planning Group's operational efficiency is a multiple of the lumbering giants, allowing for quick pivots when necessary. As anyone in the industry knows, quick pivots have been the law of the financial jungle during the past fifteen years, and they've grown more abundant since about the Ides of March 2020.

Of course, anyone whose prime motivation is monetary could take a different path: they could get on the big firm merry-go-round and jump from horse to horse. You probably know some advisors who have secured big free agent offers to move their books from one firm to another. A big wirehouse dangled $2.1 million over eight years to Daren if he agreed to switch teams and maintain his production.

It is tempting for many people to bounce from firm to firm collecting the mega-signing bonus, but think about what it suggests about the value of a broker with a solid book of business. Suppose an insurance giant or brokerage powerhouse will pay you a quarter of a million plus bonuses annually. In that case, you're worth at least half a million plus some multiple of the bonuses. Truthfully, the brokers who auction themselves to the highest bidder every few years are selling themselves short, doing little for their clients (despite the yarn they will spin as they move assets from one account to another), and simply rearranging the deck chairs on their personal Titanic.

So, Are You Ready?

Now, you have all the criteria to decide whether you're in the frame of mind to make a momentous life decision.

How to Know If You're Ready to Take the Leap

• Are you unhappy more than one-fifth of your time on the job? If so, you're in the divorce zone.

• Does the company culture, the one by which they live, not the one written on the break room wall, clash with your ethos? It's hard to live that way for long.

• Do you want to continue dividing the pie and getting the smaller slice, or are you more interested in baking the pie yourself? You're ready to be independent.

• Do you feel you're not serving your clients to the best of your ability because employer requirements don't align with their best interests? Do them a favor and transition to a true fiduciary arrangement.

• Do you still have stars in your eyes over that decadent all-expenses-paid cruise up the Danube you earned for meeting product sales requirements? Maybe leaving isn't the best choice for you right now.

• Are your emotional well-being, family life, and commitment to behave ethically just as important to you as the monetary compensation? Taking the plunge won't reduce your income; it will just reduce its importance compared to those other things.

• Are you ready to forsake your coworkers (or be forsaken by them), work like the Tasmanian Devil for a few months, and suffer a few psychological bumps and bruises before reaching the promised land of independence? The emotional commitment to the process reduces risk to near zero.

• Are you committed to following our direction? Then let's go.

We know you're out there, so this book's for you.

Does what we have described sound familiar to your situation? Are you ready to change but need help figuring out where to start? We were standing at the same intersection not so long ago, facing the same trepidation you face today. The difference is that you have us to guide you across this treacherous passage. We will give you all the information you need to get you to Leave Day.

It's all about manifesting your destiny. Let's clarify what you're leaving and where you're heading because clients want to be part of something good. Let's determine the chassis type upon which to construct that vision. We'll reveal the options and pitfalls in moving forward and mitigate the variables that lead to failure.

We'll paint you a picture of what you would be doing now if you were independent today. We'll arm you with the right questions, like what you can and can't take from the old firm, a plan to execute, and the mindset to adopt. Buckle your seatbelt and hold onto your hat. It's going to be a wild ride.

But first, let's look at something you might not have had access to back when you had stars in your eyes.

CHAPTER 2

BREAKING DOWN THE BUSINESS MODELS

*It's funny. All you have to do is say something
nobody understands, and they'll do
practically anything you want them to.*

—J. D. SALINGER, *THE CATCHER IN THE RYE*

If you're reading this book as a financial advisor, grappling with the labyrinth of the financial services realm, you are likely familiar with the sentiment we are about to explore. Daren's transition from a career in organizational development to the world of financial planning exemplifies this journey. Joining a prestigious brokerage, he was a beacon of enthusiasm, believing wholeheartedly that his mission was to secure his clients' futures, one portfolio at a time. Daren embarked on his professional journey with unwavering dedication and immersed himself in learning every facet of the business—financial planning intricacies, client relationships, and the cultivation of his clientele.

His resolve to absorb copious knowledge and excel in his profession was unwavering. He thrived on the challenge and the ever-evolving landscape of the financial services sector.

Yet, at the heart of Daren's endeavors was an unwavering commitment to serving and advocating for his clients' best interests. However, as his understanding deepened, the stark realities of operating within the brokerage world grew increasingly difficult to reconcile. Beneath his optimism lay a far more complex and challenging reality, filled with ethical dilemmas that tested his resolve.

Daren's Perspective

The early years were a whirlwind, concealing the inherent conflicts of interest beneath the sheen of clients' initial enthusiasm. I was admittedly blind to the conflicts lurking beneath the surface, overshadowed by the euphoria of new beginnings. In a landscape starved of reliable information, exploring alternative financial advising methodologies was akin to navigating a dense fog.

The industry was fraught with pitfalls, with brokerages and insurance agents vying for dominance, each peddling their wares with little regard for the consequences. It took years of piecing together fragmented insights from disparate sources, sporadic conversations, and the occasional trade publication to fully grasp the industry's true nature.

As I delved deeper, I became a self-taught expert in deciphering the intricate web of nuanced business models—from insurance agents to broker-dealers, RIAs, and the hybrid monstrosities that straddled the line between independence and servitude, each with their own self-serving agenda.

Brokerage firms emerged as the epitome of Wall Street's profit-driven machinery, prioritizing the sale of financial products over genuine client welfare. Meanwhile, insurance agents peddled insurance as a panacea for all financial woes.

Despite the facade of independence touted by modern broker-ages, dually registered independent firms merely echoed the structures of their Wall Street counterparts, blending financial manufacturing with a semblance of autonomy. The emergence of broker hybrids further muddied the waters, blurring the lines between fiduciary duty and profit-driven brokerage.

While at the firm, I encountered a deliberate lack of education on alternate business models, but who am I kidding? Brokers, driven by profit motives, prioritize their interests over client welfare. This cal-culated ignorance extends beyond my firm; it's an industry-wide phe-nomenon. Companies intentionally keep their employees uninformed to maintain control, preventing them from exploring better alternatives.

I realized the extent of their manipulation when my firm restricted interactions with advisors from other companies. This isolation mirrors the tactics of authoritarian regimes, perpetuating a distorted superiority while withholding contrasting information.

Despite the allure of lucrative incentives, I eventually realized the compromise wasn't worth it. I chose to break free from the shackles of the brokerage world, driven by a desire for ethical alignment rather than financial gain.

Change begins with questioning the status quo, even when the answers are uncomfortable. Ignorance may offer temporary comfort, but it stagnates progress. This book aims to illuminate the shadows of ignorance within our profession. While employers may prefer us to remain uninformed, knowledge empowers us to make informed decisions. Let's unravel the complexities within these pages together.

This actuality is not negligent on the part of the companies. The deliberate concealment of information within corporate entities is mere oversight—a calculated strategy to keep employees in the dark. Companies meticulously orchestrate a state of ignorance among their workforce, shielding them from alternative arrangements that might challenge the superiority of their own models. My own experiences underscored this reality vividly.

During my tenure, my firm whisked me across the country to meet with fund families and acquaint myself with their products. Yet, they barred me from engaging with advisors at competing firms. It was a systematic effort to perpetuate our ignorance about potentially better alternatives in the industry. This isolation was akin to working for an automotive giant like Ford and being barred from interacting with counterparts at Toyota or General Motors for fear that you would discover that competitors had better processes, pay scales, or customer service models. It sounds a little insane on its face, and in the apparent sense, it was. Yet, it's oddly accepted.

I now comprehend the motives driving this orchestrated ignorance—and why the big firms went to such great lengths to perpetuate it—an insatiable desire to instill blind faith in the superiority of their business model. They wanted us to drink only *their* Kool-Aid concerning the superiority of their model, approach, culture, investments, and so on. It was akin to living in a communist state where citizens are brainwashed on the virtues of an idea by a robust propaganda system and denied access to contrary information.

However, our propaganda tools served the ultimate in capitalism—we were incentivized to make boatloads of money for them, and, in turn, we made boatloads of money for ourselves. Eventually, the money became too good to rock the boat. Yet, despite the allure of substantial financial gain, the compromise proved untenable. Despite making tons of money by the time I chose to leave the brokerage world,

I knew deep down the compromise was not worth the paycheck, so I made a change.

You may be wondering, if we lived in these insular worlds enforced by the paranoid politburo in corporate headquarters, how did we learn about the alternatives?

Carmine's story embodies this profound awakening. His pursuit of knowledge, ignited by his collaboration with a business coach in 2008 and interactions with a network of independent advisors, shattered the veil of ignorance that once clouded his vision. Seeking external perspectives and witnessing advisors genuinely advocating for their clients' best interests sparked a seismic shift in Carmine's worldview.

This pivotal experience pried Carmine's eyes open, aligning with his growing unease regarding the delicate balance between serving his clients and tending to his family's needs. He gradually realized that his professional pursuits were shackled to a system where preserving his financial rewards and affiliations necessitated compromising his integrity. It dawned on him that maintaining quotas and pleasing the company often required him to prioritize sales over the genuine well-being of his clients, forcing Carmine to work with clients that were not ideal to his practice in order to sell them insurance products.

When you start asking questions and find that the answers leave you unsettled, it sets in motion a chain reaction of transformation. Far too often, we cocoon ourselves in a false sense of security, opting to disregard the uncomfortable truths that confront us. Change is a formidable force, demanding courage and resilience to break free from the clutches of ignorance. When answers no longer suffice, change becomes inevitable. Let's not consign ourselves to the darkness of ignorance—let this book be our beacon of enlightenment.

We, however, don't want anyone else to live in a dark hole of ignorance about our profession. While your employer may prefer to keep you in the dark, this book stands as a beacon of knowledge, guiding us to unravel the complexities of our field right here, right now. Together, let us decipher the mysteries and emerge stronger, armed with understanding and clarity.

Commissioned Nonfiduciary, Fee-Based, and Fee-Only

Let's explore the intricacies often overlooked by many financial professionals: the distinctions between nonfiduciary, fee-based, and fee-only models.

In the realm of financial services, the modus operandi for insurance agents and registered representatives revolves around the concept of "suitability." They recommend financial products they deem "suitable" for their clients, earning commissions (and often bonuses) through transactions. Yet, herein lies the disconnect: these agents benefit from buying and selling specific instruments, sometimes proprietary, regardless of whether they truly serve the client's best interests.

The commissions involved are often invisible or opaque to the client, buried within convoluted statements that fail to highlight the full extent of fees.

Instead, statements disclose certain fees while frequently burying additional (and often substantial) fees within the dense, convoluted fine print. These transactions might not always align with the client's best interests; in fact, we know that transactional costs can have detrimental effects on client portfolios. Therefore, the more activity within the client's account, the more likely the client's financial well-being will suffer.

Furthermore, these insurance and brokerage commissioned agents are enticed with lucrative bonuses and extravagant incentives for peddling high-profit instruments, fostering a culture where transactional gains supersede genuine client welfare. This ethos, or lack thereof, undermines the mere essence of morality, as the emphasis shifts from building lasting client relationships to driving sales figures. The incentives are purely transactional and sales-based, while the rhetoric is about relationships. This fundamental disconnect is questionable at best, of course. Still, it can get lost in the fog of battle—the battle to earn that delicious-looking vacation to Tahiti that the company dangles before its sales force.

It's essential to tread carefully here. While acknowledging the well-intentioned individuals within Wall Street giants, we must confront a system engineered to line the pockets of financial institutions operating under the cloak of "suitability." After all, once upon a time, when the Department of Labor planned to force all the advisors to act in the "best interest" of their clients when handling retirement money, annuity sales were slashed overnight.

Clients often find solace in these arrangements, shielded from the true extent of their advisor's earnings and unaware of potentially superior investment options. As we often assert, if clients are unaware of their fees, they likely surpass their expectations. The commission-based structure often leaves clients unknowingly forfeiting substantial sums, as the system intentionally obscures these realities.

A survey by the Financial Industry Regulatory Authority's (FINRA) Investor Education Foundation sheds light on the pervasive lack of transparency, revealing that a significant portion of investors (31 percent) remain oblivious to their investment fees.[2] Many (60 percent) fail to grasp the costs associated with financial professionals' advice, highlighting a concerning trend of uninformed decision-making within the financial realm.[3]

These percentages don't add up, as someone might fall into two of the three categories. Still, it is evident that most investors consulting a financial professional are entirely unaware of what it costs them—if they are even aware that they are paying.

Carmine's Firsthand Account

When starting my career, a friend steered me toward a prominent insurance company where the local manager oversaw a sizable team of over thirty agents. It quickly became apparent that my aspirations to become a CERTIFIED FINANCIAL PLANNER™, prioritizing a meticulous planning process and adhering to stringent ethical standards, were at odds with the company's ethos. My manager incessantly questioned my desire to pursue the CFP® designation, asserting that true client service was synonymous with selling the company's purportedly superior products.

And to sweeten the deal, the company dangled extravagant, all-expenses-paid vacations as rewards for peddling these products, which conveniently lined the company's coffers with hefty profits. While some of these products often did benefit the customer, that was merely a serendipitous side effect. (OK, truthfully, I didn't use the term "serendipitous side effect" myself. Daren gave me that line and spelled it for me. I'm pretty sure we don't have serendipity in New Jersey. Sometimes we're lucky, though.)

The primary function of these products was to boost the company's stock performance by a fraction of a cent. When I reached my breaking point, exacerbated by the company quadrupling its product sales quotas, I decided to bid farewell to the behemoth insurance outfit. My manager's dismissive response, suggesting I explore unscrupulous tactics, like selling off clients' bond holdings to fund whole-life policies (what the company deemed "bond alternatives"), was the final straw.

The company's fixation on life insurance as a panacea for every financial woe was absurd—akin to the proverbial hammer and nail scenario where every problem was treated as if it were a nail. We used to joke that if your knee hurt, you could rub some whole life insurance on it, and you'd feel better. The pervasive cloud of cognitive dissonance (thanks for that psychological construct, Daren!) that enveloped my colleagues failed to sway my conscience; I refused to succumb to the allure of easy profits at the expense of ethical integrity.

At that point, my resignation was a done deal (or what Daren would call a fait accompli). The depressing climate in which we operated convinced all my colleagues that this was a reasonable way to go through life. I'm happy to say that my conscience was not so easily bamboozled.

Fee-only advisors represent a departure from the traditional commission-based model embraced by agents. Their fees are explicitly disclosed at the outset, typically as a percentage of total assets under management—and are deducted directly from the client's portfolio. While alternative structures such as fee-for-service, subscriptions, hourly, or flat fees have gained traction in recent years, we'll simplify by grouping them together at one end of the spectrum. The debate over which approach best serves clients is an ongoing one.

This model offers several distinct advantages. It is a vastly superior arrangement for several reasons. First and most prominent is the transparency it affords. Clients are fully aware of their financial advisor's fees, enabling them to gauge whether the value justifies the cost. The usual fee amounts to 1 percent of a client's assets under management. Thus, for a family with a portfolio worth a million dollars, the annual fee would be $10,000. While this may seem substantial, contributing 1 percent of added value to a portfolio of such magnitude is relatively straightforward for a competent financial advisor. Indeed, there are instances where, in just a single day, I have assisted a client in earning an additional 1 percent or prevented them from making a mistake that could have resulted in a 1 percent loss.

It's important to recognize that the $10,000 we charge is only a small fraction of what a large insurance company or brokerage extracts from a million-dollar portfolio annually; it's simply concealed within spreads, margins, and kickbacks. By engaging an independent fee-based advisor, you avoid paying for extravagant office towers, relentless television advertising campaigns, or the hefty CEO salaries typical of big insurance companies or brokerages. A closer look at company payouts to advisors, which we'll explore more later, reveals significant disparities between major national companies and independent brokerages.

The second reason investors should choose to work with an advisor who charges a fee, not commissions, is the dovetailing of interests. Under this arrangement, the financial advisor increases their income when the client's assets grow and earns less when their value declines. Their fortunes rise and fall in tandem; thus, clients can trust that their advisor is financially incentivized to act in their best interest. Moreover, the financial advisor has no vested interest in generating transactions or selling proprietary products that don't enhance the portfolio's value. With interests aligned, the fee-based financial advisor always serves the client's best interest.

A message to the fee-only crew. We're not trying to dismiss your argument that "fee-only" is cleaner. We also have a perspective that suggests "fee-only" and "fee-based" offer trade-offs. Neither is superior; let's first work to end the commission-based "suitability" issue, and then we can fight over fee-only versus fee-based. We can be allies for the time being.

You may have noticed that we muddied the waters by talking about fee-only advisors at the start and fee-based advisors at the end. We did this because the Certified Financial Planning Board stipulates that anyone who sells insurance, has an insurance license, or works in the same company as someone with an insurance license cannot call themselves fee-only. Insurance products spin off commissions. Why is that an issue?

Insurance commissions are an issue because they create an inherent conflict of interest. We do believe asset protection is critical to any financial plan. Fortunately, insurance products are becoming more transparent, and fee-based options are becoming available. However, these fee-based options do present their own issues. When appropriately employed, insurance can be a valuable tool in a financial plan. (We also rarely sell annuities, which we are generally allergic to, but occasionally feel that they may be valuable to a client in a narrow set of circumstances, particularly one requiring a guaranteed payout in retirement. When we do use them, we use a fee-based option.)

The bottom line is that anyone who could experience an adverse event and could go bankrupt should have insurance to protect their assets. Homeowners insurance, life insurance, long-term care insurance, and other products all have a place in most financial plans, including ours. We're both breadwinners and fathers who want their wives and children protected if something happens to us. A financial advisor not considering insurance as part of a client portfolio is probably only partially doing their job.

The problem with insurance is that it is often sold and classified as a financial instrument rather than one providing asset protection. These sorts of products pop up periodically, such as whenever the CEO of a big insurance company has a payment coming due on their yacht. The products are designed to enhance the corporate bottom line and provide agents in the field with something new to sell to clients, emphasizing all the fancy bells and whistles attached without mentioning the hefty fees they will yield. Thus, the financial regulators exempted insurance from the fee-only claim.

Fee-based advisors represent a departure from the traditional commission-based model embraced by insurance agents. However, they can also sell insurance products as long as they are not variable products for which they receive commissions. Again, eliminating these options from the menu of services we can offer our clients strikes us as contrary to their best interests. If we find a financial instrument that is in our client's best interest we will advise the client to purchase irrespective of whether it delivers a commission to us; this represents a minuscule percentage of our income. The difference is a fee-based advisor has to "act in the best interest" at all times instead of abiding by the "suitability" standard. There can be no holidays in this standard.

Some advisors want to keep their hands pristine and be able to maintain the claim that they are fee-only. We understand that position and certainly are much more simpatico with them than with commission brokers. We feel that they are punting on a critical element of their client's financial plans and not offering expertise that would benefit their clients. We build our books of business on deep personal relationships, and our clients know we would never steer them wrong on insurance.

Even if it were merely a matter of enlightened self-interest rather than our genuine concern for our client's well-being, it hardly makes sense for us to jeopardize our relationship on a tiny commission when nearly every penny we earn is fee-based. As a fee-based advisor, you don't get to take a holiday from acting in the client's best interests when discussing insurance. We also know many fee-only advisors who partner with an insurance professional to address their client's protection needs. This model works very well because agents who only sell insurance tend to be specialists and know a lot about the ever-changing product options.

Both of us are fee-based, not fee-only. We recognize the critical role insurance plays in a well-balanced portfolio and will advise our clients about the best products for their needs. It is not exactly rocket surgery. After all, we figured it out—that any sound financial plan rests on five pillars:

Five Pillars of Financial Planning

1. Investments and savings
2. Retirement
3. Risk management
4. Estate planning
5. Tax planning

For each client, we do a deep dive into each pillar and ensure they're firing on all cylinders. That discovery process includes insurance—most fee-only advisors ignore it; some will analyze their client insurance and refer out to get policies as needed.

We've taken a tangent in our discourse on the difference between a commissioned agent and a fee-based (or fee-only) advisor, but there is one more important reason to prefer the fee arrangement.

The Four Types of Financial Service Affiliations

There, you have the three broad categories of financial professionals. Within that, a few distinctions are worth understanding regarding the types of financial companies an advisor might affiliate with.

INSURANCE COMPANIES

Typically, insurance agents work under an insurance company, but you can also be a financial advisor and offer advisory services, just like Carmine did. They get excellent training in their products but no others. They face voluminous product sales requirements to maintain their contracts and benefits, and because they work for large bureaucracies, there are extreme limitations on the agility of their technology.

Insurance companies are financial services companies that trade in various financial products, such as annuities, mutual funds, and other securities. Agents are salespeople first. They are also not fiduciaries; they work on commissions. Advisors at insurance companies are fiduciaries to their clients but only on advisory services, not with insurance sales. In fact, the company Carmine was affiliated with allowed you to become an advisor (work in your client's best interest) only if you sold enough of their insurance products.

WIRE HOUSE/BANK CHANNEL

These are full-service brokerages that provide a comprehensive range of services, such as investment banking, trading, and wealth management. Clients' assets are custodied at the wirehouse, and advisors are typically considered employees of the wirehouse or bank. The company disseminates research and financial information and provides a chassis on which all advisors can add customized products for clients. These companies offer proprietary products in addition to cross-selling various other financial instruments. The advantage for the consumer is that they can purchase multiple financial products through one broker. Yet, they must come from the wirehouse's menu of services even if a product outside that menu best serves the client.

From the employee's standpoint, wirehouses offer security and a solid foundation from which to work. But brokers pay for that security, capturing, on average, 40 percent of their revenue.[4]

HYBRID BROKER-DEALERS/RIA-ADVISORS

These asset managers usually have their Series 7 licenses, allowing them to sell commissionable products like annuities and mutual funds and still offer advisory services. To do so, they must affiliate with a broker-dealer. This affiliation is comparable to a franchise arrangement or a real estate broker situation, where the financial advisor is independent but has the power of the broker-dealer/RIA behind them. We will get into this more in chapter 3, but this hybrid model is a good alternative for those who want to work independently but prefer the security of the mothership. In this environment, your regulatory requirements must check the box for FINRA and the Securities and Exchange Commission (SEC).

REGISTERED INVESTMENT ADVISORS (RIAS)

RIAs must, by law, act in a fiduciary capacity and thus are held accountable for working unconditionally for the client's best interests, even at the short-term expense of their own financial interests. RIAs must register with the SEC or their state securities regulator and disclose any possible conflicts of interest to their clients. RIAs have more autonomy than everyone. These financial advisors are true fee-based/fee-only client advocates who must obtain Series 65 or 66 licenses to practice their trade. There is no broker-dealer relationship and no commissions paid for investment vehicles.

How Carmine's Company, a Fee-Based RIA, Works with Clients

A couple, ages forty-five and forty-three, comes to us with minimal assets but three kids to put through college. They want to know how to save enough to pay for school and still retire. This question is ridiculous in one sense—think about the pathology in an educational system where college costs six figures—but an important one, especially if you want your children to have opportunities in our knowledge-based economy. Furthermore, given the state of Social Security and the size of our nation's debt load, saving robustly for retirement is more imperative than ever.

The first thing we do is collect data because no matter what customer-focused business you're in—therapy, real estate, website design, car sales, whatever—the first and most crucial step is to listen to the client and understand their needs and desires. We do a top-to-bottom assessment of their financial statement, giving them a clear and unadulterated State of the Union address. After the evaluation, everyone is on the same page about where they stand. This first step is undoubtedly necessary because if your GPS doesn't know where you are, it can't give you directions to where you're going.

The next step is to determine the destination. What does the client want to achieve? What is critical, and what would merely be nice to have? How much are they willing to sacrifice or risk to get there? Again, this is important because if you don't know where you are going, any road will get you there.

Once we have a precise picture of the destination, we can reverse engineer the savings and investments most likely to help them reach those goals. The client may not love what we find—many people who have not yet begun planning their financial lives find themselves with substantial work to do to reach their goals. But at least we clarify how far behind they are and what will be required to get there.

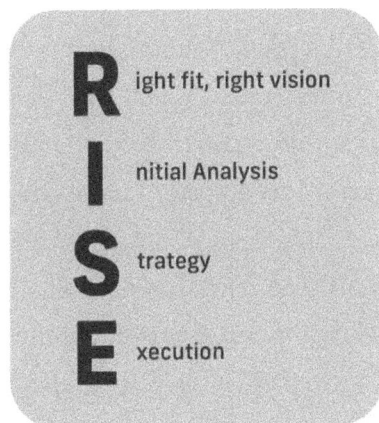

R ight fit, right vision

I nitial Analysis

S trategy

E xecution

We have a proprietary tool that automates some of this process that we call *RISE—Right* fit, right vision (to ascertain up front whether we're the right advisors for them), *Initial* analysis, *Strategy*, and *Execution*. We run Monte Carlo simulations to determine the probability in percentage terms that they will succeed in reaching their goals. By enunciating for our clients the roadblocks they will face, guiding them to wise decision-making as conditions change, and offering our expertise about the best mix of savings, investments, and protection to suit their needs, we achieve great fulfillment when their starting point of 0 percent chance of success turns into a high probability thanks to our established plan.

We do not tell our clients what to do with their money. Our job is to show them the full array of options, help them understand the impact of their decisions, offer guidance when they request it, and execute their decisions in the most efficient manner possible. Of course, our job is never-ending because the only constant in life is change.

In the case of the couple above, they were like many new clients who entered with a 0 percent chance of success, given what they had been doing to plan their financial future, which was mostly nothing. Starting at that age, with children already in middle and high school, presents daunting challenges and almost guarantees that the children will not be going to out-of-state or private universities absent substantial scholarships. But as things currently stand, if they follow our plan, which they seem inclined to do, they have a better than 80 percent chance of success.

No one is ever at 100 percent because family tragedy can interfere, Social Security could disappear, taxes could double, the dollar's value could collapse, and a whole host of even harder-to-envision circumstances could divert their plan from success. But notwithstanding some black swan events, they are in good shape.

Now that my colleagues and I have developed a relationship with the couple, connected on LinkedIn, seen photos of their kids, and followed their achievements now that we consider them friends and clients, the fees we will earn from their business will pay the bills. Still, the gratitude we feel knowing that we have the expertise to help them achieve their personal goals fills our souls. We were earning the fees the old way but losing our souls. This approach feels so much better.

There's more than one way to find a better life after being hired by a big firm. Determining the best way for you will take an honest look at what's out there and what you'll be happier doing. We'll break it all down in the next chapter.

CHAPTER 3

START YOUR OWN OR BOLT-ON?

⊂⊃⊂⊃⊂⊃⊂⊃⊂⊃⊂⊃⊂⊃⊂⊃⊂⊃⊂⊃⊂⊃⊂⊃⊂⊃

*I knew that if I failed, I wouldn't regret that, but I
knew the one thing I might regret is not trying.*

—JEFF BEZOS, FOUNDER AND CEO OF AMAZON

⊂⊃⊂⊃⊂⊃⊂⊃⊂⊃⊂⊃⊂⊃⊂⊃⊂⊃⊂⊃⊂⊃⊂⊃⊂⊃

You've made the psychological leap: coming to terms with your inability to reconcile the constant demands from above to turn your friends, family, and valued customers into cutting boards on which you carve out your slice. You're ready to take that bold step into the unknown, confident you can do good and do well simultaneously. Your family is on board for the wave you're about to ride, and you've put a few shekels away to weather any storms. You are committed to putting the large firm in the rearview mirror.

You're steeled for that, no matter how you go about this—unless it involves reassessing the nature of existence while cloistered in a monastery. There is a lot on your plate that will drain you emotionally. You're processing all this, dotting all your "I's" and crossing all your "T's." But before you get rolling, there is something you must first determine.

Who Are You?

We're not questioning your relevance or riffing on the Who; what kind of person are you? Some people are introverts; others are extroverts. Some people are outdoor enthusiasts; others are avid homebodies. Some people live by their emotions, while others live by logic. Our internal software's code and nurtured environment determine our strengths and weaknesses, likes and dislikes, fears, and desires.

For example, many introverts report that while they can spend hours being gregarious and socializing with others, they find the experience draining. After a long session of networking, introverts need to decompress. Extroverts get jazzed by socializing and generally leave a social situation wanting nothing less than more socializing. (Of course, many people are somewhere in between.) It would be unwise to thrust an introvert into one social situation after another, even if they appeared adept at it. However, that is impossible to avoid if you're unaware of the kind of internal software that individual has.

For your break from servitude, you must first ascertain which qualities you have and which you lack that might affect your success at going independent. This self-reflection is a moment for honesty about oneself.

Do you want to be an entrepreneur and own everything, including the headaches, or an intrapreneur where you're responsible for your earnings but you pay someone else to run the business and deal with all the gnat bites of everyday business ownership?

Do you want all the problems, most of the glory, and a more significant chunk of the profit, or do you want to outsource the business operations, freeing you to concentrate on advising your clients?

Do you want to own your own restaurant or run a Burger King franchise, where the company provides the recipe for French fries and Whoppers, lends you its brand, advertises on your behalf, provides software for billing and human resources, and the like, takes its cut, and demands you follow company-specific guidelines?

In the first case, where you want to be the boss, it's time to start your own Independent RIA. In the second scenario, you should bolt-on with an independent RIA firm like the two we operate.

It's a big decision you must make before you take flight. So, who are you?

One way we determined who we are was to take a DiSC® personality assessment. Daren is a big fan of utilizing this tool to help understand one's sense of self. Lots can be discussed about this model, but here is a high-level overview. As described by DiSCprofile.com, "DiSC® is an acronym that stands for the four main behavioral styles outlined in the DiSC model of personalities … D stands for Dominance, i stands for Influence, S stands for Steadiness, and C stands for Conscientiousness."[5]

DiSC® Overview[6]

"*D = Dominance:* A person primarily in this DiSC quadrant places emphasis on accomplishing results and 'seeing the big picture.' They are confident, sometimes blunt, outspoken, and demanding."

"*i = Influence:* A person in this DiSC quadrant places emphasis on influencing or persuading others. They tend to be enthusiastic, optimistic, open, trusting, and energetic."

"*S = Steadiness:* A person in this DiSC quadrant places emphasis on cooperation, sincerity, loyalty, and dependability. They tend to have calm, deliberate dispositions, and don't like to be rushed."

"*C = Conscientiousness:* A person in this DiSC quadrant places emphasis on quality and accuracy, expertise and competency. They enjoy their independence, demand the details, and often fear being wrong."

"No DiSC style is 'better' than any other, and we all use each of the four styles as we go about our daily lives. DiSC simply helps us find out which style we tend to gravitate toward most—our comfort zone. With that knowledge, we can understand our underlying tendencies and preferences and adapt our behaviors to interact with others more effectively."[7] For instance, if you're a 'D' (Dominance) type, you might find it beneficial to tone down your directness when dealing with more 'S' (Steadiness) types, who prefer a more cooperative approach.

You can take the DiSC® profile assessment or one of dozens of other personality profile tests and determine whether you are destined to be a CEO or an independent advisor. You probably already know which sounds like a more comfortable fit for you, and your gut instinct is an excellent guide. When the two of us independently took the DiSC® assessment, it told us what we already knew about ourselves: we are both tailored to run our own shops. Daren is a strong D, confident and bottom-line oriented, and Carmine is a strong i. Take a look at what his report says about him:

Carmine likes to deal with people in a favorable social environment. He does not like other managers looking over his shoulder.

If that doesn't scream "Run your own shop!" we don't know what will. And so that is what we set out to do. We select people for their cultural (values alignment) and personality fit with the rest of the firm. There is plenty of room in the marketplace for us all to prosper. Our firms attract advisors who appreciate how our corporate culture values integrity, empathy, and conscientiousness, and we seek out advisors for whom these are inherent values.

Another consideration concerning the form your departure should take is the amount of assets you have under management. If it's over $100 million and you're adept at business, it could make sense to become an independent RIA. You must register with your state if you manage less than $100 million in assets. This nightmare is on par with probating a contested will in another state during COVID with an incompetent judge and no internet access, except with the state regulatory filing, and there is no payoff in the end.

Compared with state filings, which are difficult to comply with, time-consuming, and costly, an SEC filing is a stroll in the park through fields of lavender on a sunny day. (Well, not really, but it is somewhat more straightforward). Imagine something so Byzantine that it makes an SEC filing look like a cakewalk. That is a state filing. In that case, you're likely well advised to bolt-on with an RIA until you grow your book of business to over $100 million. Keep in mind if you're under $100 million, you must register with the states you do business in; yes, that's plural—state(s).

Some financial advisors chafe at the idea that they aren't best suited for running a business, but they should understand that this is normal. Most advisors are great at advising, but lousy business owners are not cut out to be entrepreneurs. If you're not sure, read the book *E-Myth* by Michael E. Gerber.

Being an advisor and running an advisory business are two different skill sets and mindsets, with little correlation between them. Just because you can bake cakes doesn't mean you should be the one selling them. Being adept at listening and helping a client plan, matching financial instruments with client needs, anticipating the market, and guiding families to sound decision-making have little to do with opening, structuring, and marketing a business and managing employees. It's not just that being an entrepreneur is only for some; it's hardly for anyone.

Half of all companies fail in their first five years; 300,000 enterprises go belly-up annually. The odds that you're a great financial advisor and a great business operator are slim, and it's essential to understand your signature skills before you join the wrong half of businesses. Keep in mind most small businesses fail within five years for one reason or another. We're not trying to scare you; it's just important you are very self-aware about your skill set. The cards are not necessarily stacked in your favor. This is why there are around 260,000 financial advisors in the United States[8], but there are just under 15,000 independent RIA firms.[9] The people cut out for the entrepreneur role are outliers. It takes a unique combination of skills, personality, and masochism to be an entrepreneur. Some people get joy from all the heartache of owning a business, and others only see misery.

Let's face it: there is a certain appeal to being a superb money manager and concentrating solely on that. Many professionals in our field break free of the golden handcuffs but say, "I don't want to worry about the twenty-five pieces of technology I have to buy to build my own firm. I'm okay giving up a little revenue and bolting-onto an existing entity that offers all this." You must decide if you're drawn to the packaged product or if you're an entrepreneur who wants to start your own entity from scratch.

Daren's Experience Leaving the Big Brokerage

Here's how Daren described his need to carve out his own path:

I don't like someone else telling me what to do with my day. If I am inclined to something, I try it and expect to learn at least. I love being a CEO, working with advisors, and leading my staff. I am comfortable firing on all cylinders. He equated this to someone who wants to own a restaurant: they must be willing to decide on the interior paint color, consider a variety of menu designs, and spend time comparing pasta providers. But it also involves big-picture decisions, like what kind of food the restaurant will serve and what ambiance it should offer.

I'll be honest: even after careful consideration, I was fearful and wondered whether I would be successful. You're taking a leap from one ledge across a canyon to another, but the canyon is densely covered in fog, and you must determine where the ledge is on the other side of the divide. It is a leap of faith, and you're not taking it alone but with a family that relies on you. I understand why so many are hesitant to jump. For me, it's this leap that invigorates my soul; it's what fires me up. I love the high stakes that come with running your own ship.

Let's be clear that this is not an act of blind faith. To continue the metaphor of the leap, we do this knowing that the divide is small and easily broached. Because I did the research and understood the variables that would lead to success or failure, I had clients with whom I had strong relationships, and I had confidence in my ability, discipline, and work ethic to overcome obstacles and succeed. Unlike an entrepreneur who decides to open a dry-cleaning business, build an app, or start a software company, financial advisors who disengage from Global Conglomerate Enterprises, Inc. have something critical to success that should give them more confidence to launch their own enterprise: customers who value their product and service. We call this goodwill.

When you walk away, you trust in the goodwill you have created. We walk away, and generally, our customers follow us, just like a patient follows a doctor, and if you can't keep everyone you want to bring with you, it's not like you're starting from scratch. I have always had great confidence in my ability to start over from scratch because

I knew what it took to start from scratch in the first place. Don't get me wrong: many people helped me along the way, but I knew I had what it takes to re-create and reinvent should I need to.

There is a big difference between eschewing all your income for two years while you bootstrap the business and pour everything you make back into it as an app developer or software company might do and taking 75 percent of your income with you the day you walk out the door and set out your shingle.

As much as I like to congratulate myself for leaping into the swirling mists of uncertainty, the fact is that it's hard to completely fail at this endeavor, particularly if you plan for it. And if a financial advisor can't plan for his financial advisory business to succeed, he probably needs to improve at his job before considering any alternatives. The ones who fail do so because of their lack of humility and ability to discipline themselves and because they overestimate their ability to forge client relationships.

How did I plan? I had a 'Go!' binder developed over time once I realized I couldn't remain at the brokerage any longer. The law varies depending on what you're allowed to take with you when you leave, so speak with a knowledgeable attorney. But once you know you're going to leave, you would be wise to have a plan and be ready at any moment to execute it. I interviewed with every nearby firm to learn as much as possible. I studied each firm and its approach.

I learned from interviewing all the players on the street that I was exchanging one set of challenges for another by moving to another brokerage At least by going independent, I would have some control over which challenges I faced. The more due diligence I did, the clearer it became that I should go directly out on my own rather than make an intermediate transition to a hybrid broker before creating an RIA. I wanted to avoid dragging my clients through multiple transitions since I ultimately wanted to be an RIA. It was time to bolt, not bolt-on.

Nonetheless, armed with a plan, the confidence to execute it, and the belief that I could start from scratch should I need to, I was scared out of my mind. It didn't help that my wife likes certainty and was hesitant about this massive change. But I convinced her, at least intellectually, that it was the right thing to do, got the critical buy-in from her, and made the transition with her support. That is worth emphasizing: this is a team effort and impossible without your life partner on board.

How could I succeed if my wife didn't understand that the ensuing months would require my full attention to the business? She cut me much-needed slack and covered for me numerous times with the kids, and without that support, the transition would have been much more challenging. I would have felt more torn by inner conflict over my roles as husband, father, friend, and business owner than I already did.

How Carmine Achieved His Departure from the Insurance Company

Carmine's experience was similar yet entirely different.

My wife walked by me when I told her I planned to leave—this moment occurred after that safari I mentioned in Chapter 1 when I was deep inside my head and not fully present. She knew something was wrong and was unsurprised when I concluded that I had to skedaddle. She didn't even break her stride when I announced that I would make the life-changing break and establish my own firm. As she kept walking, she exclaimed that she had faith in me. I swear, that woman is a saint!

We did have a more substantive discussion later that week. It went a full minute. My wife was concerned about what might happen to our health insurance, which is a big deal when you have young kids and you're pretty sure your husband has a brain injury. We talked it out, and once I clarified that I had a plan, she was satisfied and never mentioned it again. It never was an issue, so I presume her faith was vindicated.

I spoke to a dozen advisors who had treaded the golden path to freedom and asked about their regrets, mistakes, and lessons. The same issue came up repeatedly: the advisors all said that their biggest regret was not doing it sooner, that they made a mistake not doing it sooner, and that the lesson they learned was that they should have done it sooner. That validation sealed the deal for me.

I asked them what was the worst thing that happened to them in breaking free and establishing a new enterprise. Their answers armed me with a list of issues I could easily overcome. For example, one of the advisors mentioned that he didn't document the year-end amount for an older client's individual retirement account (IRA) and, therefore, couldn't determine the required minimum distributions in advance and couldn't access the information from his former firm. That's terrible news for him and the client because it could result in a penalty equaling 50 percent of the required minimum distribution. It's a bit of oversight that could lead to a month of migraines.

For example, a client had $1 million in an IRA, and their required minimum distribution was 4 percent. That's either a $40,000 distribution or a $20,000 penalty. If you've just left a firm promising it would accrue to the benefit of your clients, losing $20,000 because of a clerical error is hardly the best way to bolster your case. Imagine that the same client travels in social circles with half a dozen other customers; it could have led to a significant loss of business for the financial advisor. (Spoiler alert: he tracked down the information, and everything worked out.)

When I heard that, I made an essential mental note: don't do that. Document the client's prior year account balances before leaving so that you know the required minimum distributions for those over age 73. Today, I counsel any advisor joining our firm who has clients over that age to save on their end the client's December statement from the prior year so that once the account gets transferred, they will know how much they are required to take this year. Warren Buffett is often credited with saying, "It's good to learn from your mistakes. It's better to learn from other people's mistakes." I'd be a genius if I learned only from my mistakes, but others have also been very accommodating.

Asking yourself who you are and digging deeply has many positive implications beyond the professional side. This book is different from that kind of book, so don't expect us to wax poetic about the power of therapy, meditation, or deep dives into the essence of your being. Each of us has a growth coach—the same one (which is how we met)—and we always consider this question. The point is that asking and answering this big question can lead to insights that help us find the right path for us and avoid one that is a bad fit.

How Do You Want to Spend Your Time?

When deciding whether to bolt-on or bolt, the next question is, how do you want to spend your time? If you would be happy as a clam spending every working minute focusing on money management, learning about new financial products, considering your client needs, meeting with them and building relationships, running various sets of numbers to uncover the best options tailored for each client, and fostering the business relationships that lead to more clients, well, good luck with that!

In actuality, the paperwork is voluminous, and avoiding it is not an option. But you can spend 80 percent of your time on financial planning and 20 percent on all the detritus that fill our professional lives, such as all the regulatory compliance and employer requirements. If that's your bag, you should bolt-on with an RIA and leave all the ancillary considerations to someone else. You can make a fine living and sleep very well at night.

If, on the other hand, you are energized by a different equation, one in which you spend 20 percent of your time servicing a smaller book of business and 80 percent of your time running a business, developing a vision, culture, and strategies for a successful enterprise; taking a disproportionate amount of the risk; and reaping a disproportionate amount of the monetary reward, then establish an RIA firm and hire qualified people from the former category. Some people prefer driving the bus, and others like riding in it while enjoying the scenery out the window. (We're not entirely sure how this analogy works, but you get the idea. We're all hardwired differently and not truly happy unless we follow our personal bliss.)

Before we move on, you need to ask yourself a question that many of those toiling for big companies can't answer: How are you getting paid? It will be tough to stay once you dig into this question and learn how the game is rigged against you and your clients. In fact, the more you learn about the industry and all the secrets hidden behind the curtain, the more the impetus to make like a banana and split.

CHAPTER 4

HOW ARE YOU REALLY GETTING PAID?

Injecting some confusion stabilizes the system.

—NASSIM NICHOLAS TALEB

You have probably heard the story of the cobbler's children. It's a metaphor for people not practicing in their personal lives what they are professionally employed to do every day. It's the website designer whose website is templated and challenging to navigate. It's the hairstylist who badly needs a haircut. It's the residential building contractor who rents an apartment. It's the financial advisor who goes bankrupt.

In the case of the cobbler, he makes shoes for everyone in the village, but his own kids run around barefoot. He lacks the time, inclination, or discipline to make shoes for his kin, even if they would be much better off if he did. The reason may be sloth, but it's more likely because employing his expertise on himself and his family (or herself and her family) isn't a moneymaking proposition.

We have seen the same thing with financial advisors. In the case of fee-based advisors who bolt-onto a brokerage, these are semi-independent intrapreneurs who run their own businesses with their own names and their own shingles out front but who leverage the brand, platform, and backroom operations of a larger company, much the way many real estate agents operate. Their primary skills are managing money and building relationships. Running a business is not a secondary skill, so much as a necessity, but is performed somewhat reluctantly and half-heartedly.

We know this because it is be the first time they have ever contemplated the issue when we ask them about their revenue and expenditures. They charge their clients the standard 1 percent of assets under management and consider little beyond that. It is hard to believe that their thinking ends there because there is so much beyond that.

The point is that they are earning—that is, taking home to buy food and clothing and a $1,000 phone every two years—significantly less than they think. More importantly, they are making decisions about their businesses without considering all the information available to them.

Many believe they are paying the brokerage one-tenth of 1 percent for each client; that is, they are forwarding 10 percent of their revenue to the large brokerage. You can decide for yourself whether that's a good deal based on all the services they receive from the company. The notion that their profit then is nine-tenths of 1 percent of client assets under management is an absurdity that should be evident to anyone who deals with numbers. (Hint: that's all of us.)

Simple multiplication and subtraction are nowhere near the end of the calculation. It isn't complicated to make sense of income and expenditures; make a spreadsheet and break down where every dollar is going. After all, the advisor may rent an office, hire and pay employees, pay office expenditures like electricity and heat, and cover many other expenditures. Once they understand how much of their 1 percent is diluted by costs, they can calculate their actual income, which will be more like half a percent or more. On $20 million under management (just as an example), that is the difference between taking home $180,000 and less than six figures.

In San Francisco, or northern New Jersey, where we live, as the purchase price of an ordinary home starts at seven figures, it's tough to buy a week's worth of lattes for that. We have been regularly shocked at the lack of accounting we see colleagues doing on their own practices. Try it for yourself; ask a quasi-independent broker at a large broker what their payout is. They will say something like 90 percent; just look at them with a slight head tilt.

That Tempting Forgivable Loan Is a Trap

Then there is that forgivable loan the brokerage dangles in front of advisors to lure them into their sticky web. They devise these loans much like the indentured servitude deals common in biblical times: the loan is only forgivable if you toe the company line (i.e., keep your production up) for some specified period, like seven years. There is no discount for coming to your senses or discovering your personal code of ethics, so leaving requires paying back the loan in full even if they fire you.

One of our friends was fired from a brokerage for a compliance lapse, and a few weeks later, he was paying the loans back. This process is how the broker-dealer gets its tentacles into advisors and prevents them from ever considering free agency. Moreover, those loans aren't company largesse; the brokerages raise their clawback rates to recapture the cost of the loan long before the end of the note.

A six-year, $100,000 forgivable loan eliminates the possibility of departure for six years. It gives the advisor two or three years of advantage before the brokerage makes a profit on the deal. On a ten-year loan, which is now more common in the industry, your first grader will be in high school by the time you can consider a change. That is considerable time spent kicking money back to your employer for the opportunity to sell products that your clients might not need. By the end of the loan, you have likely paid the brokerage twice for the amount they lent you. They are not doing it for free; they figured out how to monetize their investment. On that six-year loan, you can break even by earning 12 percent annually on the original amount. So much for free money!

This legerdemain only works if the advisor isn't closely watching how the brokerage's hands are moving the shells around. When Daren left his firm, other brokerages swooped in to entice him to move his production to them. They dangled what sounded like lottery winnings, including one offering a $2.1 million forgivable loan if he maintained his production and stayed for seven years. That they would propose to spend $300,000 annually for "production" suggests the value of their patronage is more like $600,000.

Taking that deal would have handcuffed Daren to yet another big brokerage with proprietary platform fees and exaggerated spreads that cost his clients a barely noticeable amount of their earnings on every transaction. It doesn't take long for that free money to drip away. The idea of locking myself in for seven years was just intolerable.

This arrangement also creates an inherent conflict of interest. In a vacuum, the requirement to sell more products to the universe of potential customers is merely pressure to perform. Almost every person in a sales position is pushed by their employer to sell more products, more often, to more people and to sell that company's products, not their competitors. Even customers understand that the Chrysler dealer will not sing the praises of a Hyundai and attempt to convince them to purchase one.

Sales reps make their livings this way; quotas, bonus systems, and other incentives rely on these tactics. An ad representative for a television station is endlessly incentivized to sell more ad time, online ads, and ancillary products to any business they can, whether that business has purchased ads in the past or would become a new customer.

This concept is particularly true, as in the case of the car dealer, in a transactional relationship where the buyer has little or no personal connection to the seller. But this shouldn't be the sandbox in which financial advisors play. No wonder a large percentage of Americans don't trust financial advisors. If you work for a large brokerage, you're facing pressure to sell more proprietary products to a closed system of existing customers with whom you have established a relationship based on trust, a horse of a different color. Customers of advisors put their life savings, retirement plans, and even much of their financial decision-making in the hands of their advisors and expect that as an element of that relationship, they will get helpful advice about what works best for them and their families.

Our clients rely on us to steer them around the rocks, not into them, to secure their financial future, not ours, and to earn them the highest returns on their investments, not to earn ourselves the best junket for a five-star resort in an exotic locale. To sell them products primarily so we can achieve quotas, make sales goals, and keep our forgivable loan is a transparent breach of trust. The dynamic creates an inherent conflict of interest that we could only abide by for a brief time.

If you want a window into these corporate entities' inherent conflicts, read their voluminous, 8-point-type disclosure statements, which are required by law and presented so that no one will read them. If they do, they will struggle to comprehend. These statements document the hundreds of millions of dollars the companies receive in revenue-sharing payments—incentives to sell products—from mutual funds, 529 product partners, and annuity partners. Most brokerages won't let their brokers sell any products that haven't paid to play. Don't believe us? Spend an hour with your favorite web browser typing in the phrase, "broker revenue sharing." It's all hidden in plain sight. We have shown many of our colleagues in various brokerages these disclosures, but most choose not to address the conflicts.

We pulled one disclosure from a recent prospect that had the following to say: By law, the nonfiduciary firms—those earning money via commission rather than advisory fees—must print something like the following: "The more trades in your account, the more you pay us. As a result, we have an incentive to encourage you to trade more often in your account."

There it is in black and white, but the paradoxical effect of this government mandate is that it frees the advisor from disclosing this information orally. Research shows that the percentage of people reading these legal statements is near zero.

A 2017 Deloitte survey of two thousand consumers found that 91 percent always agree to legal terms and services without reading them. For consumers under thirty-five, that is true of 97 percent.[10] A pair of researchers at York University in Toronto and the University of Connecticut ran an experiment. They created a fake social networking site and required users to sign the terms and conditions statement to access it. It included a proviso that users agree to sacrifice their first-born child. It also stipulated that their information would be shared with the National Security Agency. Not surprisingly, a mere 2 percent declined.[11]

In other words, the nonfiduciary firms know they have little to fear from the disclosures, even when they suggest that consumers could get fooled: "When we provide you with a recommendation as your broker-dealer or act as your investment adviser, we have to act in your best interest and not put our interest ahead of yours. At the same time, how we make money conflicts with your interests. You should understand and ask us about these conflicts because they can affect our recommendations and advice." We don't have any data on how many clients or prospective clients ask about these conflicts, but in our experience, it was rare.

Evidence suggests that these conflicts of interest affect the sales of financial instruments. In 2016, when the Obama administration's Labor Department established a rule requiring all financial advisors to act as fiduciaries for their clients, sales of annuities, the bane of many financial advisors who care about their clients, fell off the table. Why? Because in the absence of hefty commissions and fees for the financial advisor, there exists little justification for selling most clients' annuities.

The main benefit of annuities is the tempting 7 percent commission for the financial professional and their firm. On a $250,000 annuity, that's a nice $17,500 check. Need a down payment on a boat? Sell some sucker an annuity. Annuities are essentially fee-laden cover charges for entry into the insurance company casino, where the consumer is more likely to lose money than to win. At least in a casino, you're entertained while you lose your shirt.

We know of one company that cut its commission on annuities by one percentage point, which prompted a 40 percent decline in sales. It's not that demand slackened—almost no one comes to their financial advisor asking for an annuity. Instead, irritated registered reps and advisors of that company looked elsewhere to generate significant returns—for themselves.

The Behemoths Are Sticking It to You, Too

The big firms seek to generate boatloads of revenue at the expense of their agents and customers. Consider the case of the less-than-transparent approach in which life insurance companies and brokerages negotiate with one another concerning target premiums. Employing its proprietary assumptions and software program, a life insurance company might designate a target premium (that's a fancy word for commission payout) of $100,000 to sell the customer a policy. The insurance company negotiates with the brokerage before setting the registered rep's payout schedule. They effectively negotiate a "holdback" on some of the commissions to go directly into the broker's pocket, circumventing the sales agent.

How is this possible? Well, we don't know exactly, but it probably has a lot to do with lobbyists, opacity in the design of the financial instruments, and wink-wink, negotiations between executives. Understanding the motives of the decision-makers helps make sense of this dynamic: The executives who run the companies we once worked for are evaluated by shareholders and their boards of directors based on the revenue and profit they generate, not on how fairly and transparently they treat their customers and employees. When in doubt, follow the money.

Hybrid RIA/broker-dealers think of themselves as primarily independent advisors who occasionally dabble in commissioned sales, much like fee-based advisors who are RIAs. However, the singular difference between hybrid and fee-based RIAs is a gaping chasm. No matter how few proprietary products they sell, hybrids operate on the brokerage's proprietary platform, from which the brokerage extracts fees. The platform limits the range of products available, which may prevent the advisor from employing the product that serves the client's best interest. If there are barriers to employing the entire universe of strategies and financial instruments on behalf of clients, financial advisors can only consider themselves partially independent.

That is another way of saying that even as a hybrid, you are beholden to corporate machinations and are more conflicted in fully acting in your client's best interests, even if you have them at heart. This approach is qualitatively different from a fee-based RIA who is entirely independent even when they occasionally advise their clients to a commissionable instrument like life insurance or long-term care.

The way we look at it, our long-term interests are served by subjugating our short-term interests to those of our clients. With the guiding philosophy that what is ethically correct is always expedient, it is easy to take the ethical high road. The key is removing and mitigating as many conflicts of interest as possible, which includes eliminating conflicted organizations from influencing how you serve your clients.

For example, when Daren started his firm, an insurance company offered the new RIA a percentage of all the commissions his advisors generated, just as they do for the brokerages. It's an alluring offer.

I turned it down because that arrangement could be riddled with conflicts of interest that jeopardized the trusting relationship I'd worked hard to develop with my clients and my advisors. Running that offer through the filter of my ethos that doing what is right for my client is always long-term expedient; it's easy to refuse the kickback and pass along the discount to the client. The provider is selling their product; if that catapults it to the best option for my client, that benefits them and, therefore, me. That is the only factor we use to determine the products we choose for our clients. That is the only way our clients can fully trust us, whether they understand our decision-making process or not.

We have many friends in the business who choose to remain blind to the conflicts of interest created in this hybrid arrangement. They work as a fiduciary part of the time, perhaps even most of the time. They deliver good service to their clients and generally care about their financial success. But they are also captivated by the competition to sell more, generate more profits, win the game, see their name at the top of the leaderboard, and enjoy the benefits in their bank account. They are the salivating dogs in Ivan Pavlov's experiments on positive reinforcement. (Pavlov found that dogs began salivating when the technician who usually fed them arrived, even when he wasn't there to feed them.)

To sleep at night in the face of this inherent conflict, they employ pretzel logic, telling themselves that they work in their client's best interests most of the time and only occasionally for their family. This powerful psychological concept is called cognitive dissonance, in which we construct narratives to justify acting on how we feel, even in the face of contrary facts. Overcoming our natural inclination to fall into the haven of cognitive dissonance and changing our beliefs or behavior requires a willingness to be brutally honest with ourselves. It is a tall mountain for most people to climb, especially when money is at stake. It hasn't been easy for us either; conflicts of interest are everywhere; it takes diligence and courage to see the truth and call it what it is.

The problem with cognitive dissonance is that weak voices in our brains' nether regions whisper that we know what we're doing is wrong. Daren calls this "the voice at 2 a.m." For some people, the shouts of joy from raking in the cash drown out the whispers. For others like us, the discomfort of hearing that voice forces us to confront the raw reality and conclude that we can't live that way. We can only be happy if we spend our professional lives serving customers we genuinely value, many of whom have become our dear friends. Some of our former colleagues think we are being martyrs, but there is no sacrifice for the innumerable of independent fiduciaries out there. In the long run, we have found that we are doing better by doing good—and that little voice does not torture us. We know exactly how we are paid, for what, and why. And we can sleep soundly for the knowing.

One of the many ancillary benefits of working this way is explaining how we get paid to our clients. When we worked for the corporate behemoths, with the intersecting layers of fees, commissions, bonuses, forgivable loans, sales goals, and all that, a full accounting of our convoluted payment structure, if we could have even done it, would have taken an hour. Even a cursory explanation took Daren twenty minutes back when he was in the grip of corporate America and did more to confuse most clients than enlighten them.

Today, we are grateful that it takes a minute. It is little more than this: "You pay us a fee based on your assets under our management. The more you're worth, the more we make, so our interests dovetail. On rare occasions, we may suggest you utilize insurance for which we receive a commission. In every such case, we will disclose that to you so you can make an informed decision. We will always serve your best interests and none other."

Being transparent about our fees is freeing. The only reason to be opaque is to hide something, which requires keeping track of what we conceal and reveal. It's the same with transparency about how you get paid. Just as customers want to be informed about how their advisors get paid and what the service is costing them, advisors want transparency from corporate headquarters about how they are paid and the depth of the bite the company is taking out of their wallets.

The industry is designed to create opacity, convolution, and obfuscation—in short, to confuse you—so that more goes to the corner office and just enough goes to the foot soldiers to keep them marching. Don't believe us? Go ask the smartest person in the office to explain their compensation plan. If they get 70 percent right, they are a walking prodigy.

Keeping track of the myriad strands comprising a tangled web of opacity requires mental gymnastics and more initiative than we can muster. Plus, it can be fatiguing and angst producing, particularly if you have a conscience or are attuned to your self-deception. No thanks; that is way more work than we have the capacity to handle. We go home to our kids when we want to be constantly perplexed.

All this is to say that many advisors attached to corporate entities aren't crystal clear about how they get paid and how much more they could earn working in a different arrangement, even one less focused on the monetary bottom line and instead focused on the relational wealth that feeds the soul and ultimately feeds the bank account as well, just not of the faceless entity or its shareholders. Now that we have established the many motivations for cutting ties with the mothership and striking out on our own or with an existing independent fiduciary, as well as the many benefits once you do, the next question is, how?

How do you overcome the inertia of staying put? How do you abandon friends and coworkers? How do you detach from the iron grip that the company has on your personal and professional lives? How do you trade the security of health insurance, vacation time, and other benefits for the unknown? How do you give up the Cabo trip dream? How do you capture the information you need to retain your clients, establish a location for the new business, and prepare all the millions of minuscule details of building a business while simultaneously earning a living?

The answer is, you make a plan. In the next chapter, we will walk you through the detailed process and the countless requirements of a departure plan, many of which you would have yet to consider. We know what is required because we both asked many people who had paved that road before us and because we did it ourselves and sport arrows on our backs to show for it. We can't wait to take more in the back for publishing this book.

CHAPTER 5

BUILDING YOUR PLAN: HOW AND WHEN

A goal without a plan is just a wish.

—ANTOINE DE SAINT-EXUPÉRY

There are whole PhD theses and book sections at bookstores, to the extent that there are still bookstores, a whole wing of psychology and marketing about the science of decision-making.

We are going to boil it down to a couple of paragraphs. However, bear with us because, like our heads, there is a point.

Most of us are reasonably bad at making decisions, even major ones like whom to marry (Exhibit A: our wives married us!), which house to buy, and which career we should pursue. That is because in a nutshell—where most of our ideas belong—humans do three things that prevent them from correctly analyzing their options.

First, we are distracted by the shiny objects, allowing them to overwhelm the necessary considerations. For example, when house shopping, we are mesmerized by the infinity pool, wet bar, or gigantic backyard and fail to account for the HVAC system on its last legs, the foundation about to lose its war with gravity or the deteriorating neighborhood.

Second, we employ suboptimal strategies to simplify and expedite the decision-making process. These mental shortcuts, called *heuristics*, are filled with cognitive biases. Heuristics are great for cutting through the information that often consumes us. Yet, they are poor substitutes for examining all aspects of a situation and determining the costs and benefits of a decision.

For example, we go to the supermarket to buy pasta, and there are forty-three options from nineteen brands staring us in the face—artisanal, whole wheat, twelve-grain, locally made, generic supermarket brand, and so on. They come in different sizes, so calculating the comparative prices requires an abacus and differential equations.

To avoid all that, we choose the brand name on the middle shelf that doesn't require us to bend down or reach up on our tippy toes and pull off the shelf. This rationale is why Daren still flies Southwest and Carmine flies first class. Daren does what he knows because that's how he has always flown. Mind you, Carmine is 5'6" and Daren is 6'1". Carmine is built like a star running back, while Daren is built like a gangly giraffe.

That's heuristics.

Third, we struggle with self-awareness. What will make us happy, not just this minute but down the road? What does this decision require from us, and are we willing and able to do what it takes? If not, why not? What, exactly, are we afraid of? What biases and fears stand in the way of our success?

To overcome these roadblocks to sound decision-making, we must be honest with ourselves, honest *about* ourselves, fully informed and rational about the pros and cons. That doesn't mean there is no emotional component; quite the contrary, we need to know what drives our emotions and our ability to manage them. It doesn't matter how rational you think you are; you're still an emotional being.

All that is a prequel to every financial advisor's monumental decision about whether to leave the corporate safe haven. There are many considerations, including money, time, ethical concerns, the best interests of clients, our emotional health, and more. Most people don't make this decision on the spot or in one day; the idea simmers in our heads and hearts, slowly bubbling up. At some point, it becomes incontrovertible that we must make a change, and that is when we begin the preparations. Most people who leave of their own volition have been stewing over the decision, thinking about it, seeking counsel, laying the groundwork, and planning it for months, if not longer.

You should know that your employer has laid the same ground-work to keep you in their clutches. They replace hope and faith with fear, the most powerful emotion. Fear you will lose your clients (not if you provide good service and have built strong relationships). Fear you will lose your income, travel perks, and health benefits. (You'll replace them, of course.) Fear that your kids will go hungry, your new workplace will be toxic, the new computer system will be inadequate, and you'll regret your decision and thus be stuck in the new, unknown situation. Most brokerages strategically tell a narrative that they are there to protect you from your clients and regulators (but will hang you out to dry when push comes to shove). Because you can't be sure what comes next, all you have is the unknown. The unknown is the scariest variable we face as humans.

Fear is a powerful motivator. Our lizard brains are hardwired for it. Fear has been used as a motivator for millennia to significant effect. At the Nuremberg Trials of Nazi officials and their collabora-tors, Hermann Goering, the architect of the Gestapo and Hitler's second-in-command, revealed to prosecutors the chilling ease with which he manipulated subordinates into committing atrocities by instilling fear. We don't mean to suggest that financial firms in the twenty-first century United States are comparable in any way to that; their tactics, though, are borrowed from the same lineage.

Where initiative is required to leave, the big corporate firms exploit your natural inertia, throwing sandbags around the perimeter, increasing the effort needed to escape. They create a dependence on their computer system, their customer management system, and their reporting system. They invest in messaging that discourages departure, particularly of high performers, and lard those same rainmakers with largesse, like all-expenses-paid trips to exotic locales. They are, in effect, bribing you to keep your production with them.

Your firm is intentionally making it difficult to leave. After all, their survival depends on you remaining a cog in their wheel.

Consequently, *wanting* to leave is not enough. Before commit-ting to the independent space, you must be financially, intellectually, and emotionally ready. Your family must be on board for the leap of faith, and you must prepare for the long days ahead. Breaking free is not for the faint of heart; it requires that you trust yourself to work hard, be wise, and do the right thing.

Many financial advisors take the half step of leaving their current overseer for well-compensated indentured servitude elsewhere. They join forces with another large firm, enticed by the promise of a soft landing and comfortable conditions. Daren, for instance, was offered more than $2 million over seven years—nearly $300,000 annually—to maintain 70 percent of his production. Any competent advisor realizes that if they are willing to pay you $2 million over seven years, you must inherently be worth more than that to yourself. There is no such thing as a free lunch. By embracing the resources they offer—such as technology, marketing, and other tools—you can achieve even greater success while retaining ownership of your integrity. Let the devil seek souls elsewhere; yours is not for sale.

Strategic planning is critical for those who opt to skip the intermediary steps and dive headfirst into entrepreneurship. As you often advise your clients, failure to plan equates to planning to fail.

Now, picture the firm of your dreams—unfettered by real-world constraints, where your ideas receive instant approval. What does your ideal firm look like? Consider the services you'll offer in the coming year, the next three years, and the next decade. How large would your team be, and what cutting-edge technology would you implement? Step one is to answer these questions and make the decision to confront them head-on.

Step two entails taking concrete action—whether it's putting pen to paper or electrons to a computer file—mapping out your aspirations for the end of year one, year three, and year ten. As you project further into the future, your thoughts can be more abstract, but for year one, specificity is key, with clearly defined benchmarks along the way.

Pre-Transition Questions You Must Answer

There will be many questions beyond what we have outlined. Every situation is unique, but these should get you started.

• What data can you legally take or not take with you?

• What are the legal parameters around communication with clients at your current firm after you leave?

• If you're going to have staff, can you take your staff with you? What are the legal considerations?

• What technology will you continue to use, and what technology do you need to acquire? Can you continue to use any of your licenses for the various tech providers, and who owns that client's date?

• What is the timeline for registering with your new firm?

• Are you going to have an office? If so, where will it be?

• What will be the brand of your new firm, or will you be using someone else's?

• What provider will you use for benefits, health, life, etc.?

• If you are operating under a DBA at your old firm and would like to continue using the DBA at the new firm, who controls the domain for your website?

• Can the new custodian take custody of all the assets held at your current firm?

Pre-Transition: Bolting On

• What technology will you require, and what will be supplied by your new firm?

• What expenses will the firm be responsible for, and which will fall under your purview?

• Who will handle the billing, when will billing occur, and with what frequency?

• What are the compliance procedures for your new firm?

• How are clients' assets managed at the new firm?

• Will you receive planning assistance?

• Will office space be provided, or will you need to arrange your own?

• Will there be support staff to aid you during transitions?

• Will the new custodian cover any transfer fees, and if so, for how long?

• Are there any fees clients must pay upon departing from their previous firm?

• What is the investment management strategy of your new firm?

• Does the new firm offer coaching or additional services?

• Will your new firm assist with marketing efforts, and what are the respective responsibilities?

• Will the new firm provide leads?

Pre-Transition: Starting Your Own

Starting a new firm is very different from bolting-onto another established firm. There is no way we can make this a comprehensive list because there are so many items you need to understand to become an entrepreneur. As a baseline, you must answer these questions before you start your journey. We literally could fill an entire book just on this subject.

Questions to Answer before Starting Your Own Firm

- Will your regulatory oversight come from the state authorities or the SEC?
- Which range of services will your firm provide to clients?
- Which custodian will you select and why?
- What technological tools will you require, and how will you evaluate and select them?
- How will you safeguard your firm against cyber threats?
- Who will serve as your chief compliance officer?
- What will be your compliance framework and system?
- How will you manage client risk expectations?
- Who will handle billing and performance tracking?
- What will your investment process entail?
- Who will execute your trades to ensure optimal execution?
- Which attorney will assist with legal documentation?
- What workflows and processes will you establish?
- Where will you obtain errors and omissions (EO) Insurance?
- Who will oversee your accounting department?
- Who will manage payroll and HR if you plan to hire staff?
- Will you utilize social media platforms and archives?
- What entrepreneurial operating system will you adopt?
- Which provider will you choose for your website and branding?

- How will you generate leads for your business?
- Which bank will you partner with?
- How will you handle cash flow and financial projections?
- What email system will you utilize?
- What internal communication tools will you implement?
- Are you prepared to take on the responsibility of managing people? Do not underestimate this as it's a significant task when running a business.

As we reviewed this list, we shared a moment of laughter, recognizing the sheer madness involved in launching our own ventures in this industry. Both of us experienced a pivotal moment at the inception of our firms, prompting us to question our grip on reality. While this list is extensive, it barely scratches the surface. Venturing into entrepreneurship demands a certain level of daring and dedication—qualities possessed by those willing to invest their entire being into bringing their vision to life.

Business Planning

The initial days were an avalanche of problems and solutions, patience and understanding, and trust that everything would work out. It did, of course, but not without pools of blood, sweat, tears, and energy drinks. Some weird people (like Carmine) even opt for exercise, healthy eating, and meditation, but what's the point when coffee exists? The most surprising part was this: while we were sweating about our future, navigating the swirl of emotions, the gains and losses, the concerns about our family's financial health—amid all the toil and trouble—were some of the best times of our careers. We were building something that is ours. We were the masters of our universe.

If you have never made a business plan, and you're about ready to embark on this journey, then now is the time. There are many approaches and tools to help you effectively plan. We are not going to go into all the details here, but we will give you a basic outline. Generally, having a mission, vision, and values is baseline. Your business needs to be guided by a healthy set of key performance indicators (KPIs) to track your progress and growth. You then need to have a one-year, three-year, and five-year plan. Ten years is nice but usually abstract. In addition, you need to have a system for execution and accountability.

In case you have been sleeping for the past twenty years, here are some reasons why creating and maintaining a business plan are so critical:

- *Clarity of Vision and Goals:* When your vision is clear, decisions are easy.
- *Strategic Planning:* Where is the industry heading and are you ahead of the curve or are you about to run off the side of a mountain?
- *Long-Term Growth:* Supports long-term growth by providing a strategic framework for scaling your business over time.
- *Communication Tool:* A business plan acts as a communication tool to your employees and presents a cohesive and professional image of your business, fostering confidence and trust.

As a part of that business plan, you should clearly outline and describe the mission, vision, and values of the organization. There are lots of discussions as to how one defines these. We prefer to keep it simple.

Mission, Vision, and Values

There are many ways organizations choose to answer the mission, vision, and values questions. Like everything, we prefer to keep it simple. By being clear about these, you will be more likely to create a strong organizational culture that aligns to your vision and mission.

- *Mission:* Why are you in business?
- *Vision:* Where are you going?
- *Values:* What is important to you?

Whether you are bolting-on or starting your own, you should have a clearly defined set of mission, vision, and values. Supporting your mission should be a robust set of KPIs.

KPIs

KPIs are vital tools for any organization as they provide clear, measurable objectives against which progress can be assessed. By establishing and tracking KPIs, your business gains insight into their performance, enabling them to make informed decisions and adjustments to achieve their goals effectively. Whether you're going to be a solo practitioner bolting-on or starting your own firm, KPIs should support every role in the company.

What Should Be Included in Your Plan

A financial advisor's one-year business plan should include several key components to ensure clarity, focus, and achievable goals. Here's a breakdown of what it should entail:

- *Executive Summary:* Provide a brief overview of your business plan, outlining your objectives, target market, and key strategies.
- *Business Goals and Objectives:* Clearly define your short-term (one-year) goals and objectives. These could include targets for revenue growth, client acquisition, assets under management (AUM) increase, or expanding services.
- *Target Market Analysis:* Conduct a thorough analysis of your target market, including demographics, financial needs, and preferences. Identify niches or segments where you can add value and tailor your services effectively.
- *Competitive Analysis:* Assess your competitors' strengths, weaknesses, and market positioning. Determine how you can differentiate yourself and capitalize on opportunities in the market.
- *Service Offerings:* Define the range of services you offer to clients, emphasizing your value proposition and how it addresses their financial needs and goals.
- *Marketing and Sales Strategy:* Outline your plan for attracting and retaining clients. This may include digital marketing strategies, networking events, referral programs, and client seminars.

- *Operational Plan:* Detail the day-to-day operations of your business, including staffing requirements, technology infrastructure, compliance procedures, and client communication protocols.
- *Financial Projections:* Develop realistic financial projections for the next year, including revenue targets, expenses, profit margins, and cash flow forecasts. Ensure your projections are based on sound assumptions and market research.
- *Risk Management Plan:* Identify potential risks and challenges to your business, such as regulatory changes, market volatility, or cybersecurity threats. Develop strategies to mitigate these risks and ensure business continuity.
- *Timeline and Milestones:* Create a timeline with specific milestones and deadlines for achieving key objectives throughout the year. Regularly review and adjust your plan as needed to stay on track and respond to changing market conditions.

By including these elements in your one-year business plan, you can establish a road map for success, align your efforts with your long-term vision, and effectively manage your financial advisory practice. If you're going to be adding staff to your firm, you cannot underestimate the importance of creating alignment. The first principle of alignment is having a clear road map.

We both update our business plan every year, and we identify and track what tasks and projects need to get done each quarter of the year. This keeps us and our teams focused on what's important and adds accountability to everyone.

At different times in our lives, we read the book *Traction* and immediately saw the Entrepreneurial Operating System, also known as EOS, as the framework for something very valuable. We recommend anyone who leads a business team to read that book. Carmine read it in 2007, but the timing was not right for him to implement. He read it again in 2018 and knew the timing was right to start utilizing.

If you prepare for this hierarchy of concerns, you will not be disappointed that the first six months can't possibly be a period of growth. You're building the vehicle and can't expect it to win a race yet. If you experience revenue growth during the first six months, you have found the magic bat that hits a grand slam despite the empty bases.

The truth is, once you get past the emotional impact of separation, it's not difficult to effect the tactical change. You must give yourself time to recalibrate while life quiets down dramatically after the transition. The advisors who joined us later told us that adjusting to the new transition was not nearly as challenging as expected because our teams helped them with the process. Several new advisors were operating at full tilt within ninety days. That's possible if you're bolting-onto an independent firm but not likely if you're starting from scratch, the way we did. Your mileage may vary, but reasonable expectations are necessary to ensure future happiness.

Most financial advisors put off their planning until after they conduct their discovery. You've got to kick tires and understand all your options before you build your plan. Without due diligence, you might be climbing the wrong ladder because you don't know what your options are or what your journey will look like. "A goal without a plan is just a wish,"[12] French writer Antoine de Saint-Exupéry said.

Carmine doesn't generally quote French writers to his clients; the closest he gets to anything French is having fries with his burger. But he tells them that when the vision is clear, decisions are easy. Creating that vision will facilitate the small choices you have to make today because it will be clear what objective they are serving.

Preparing for Successes

During the transition period, it's important to focus on the small wins and not on the grueling process, the headwinds, or the setbacks. There may be a lot of drama surrounding your departure and process of establishing a competing entity, but your job is to face forward and set your gaze on the future. That means celebrating every small success so that you don't get overwhelmed with the small defeats.

When a client declines to reciprocate your announcement, celebrate all those who remained loyal. When a former coworker breaks off your friendship, celebrate those who genuinely wished you the best of luck. It's important to stack these successes one on top of the other so that you can see how high your pile of blessings is growing and avoid obsessing about the inevitable obstacles. As any politician knows, you don't have to convince everyone, just 50 percent plus one. (Presidential elections excepted.)

Because there will be setbacks, some of them are unexpected. When Daren left his firm, his colleagues took it very personally and acted accordingly. The culture of his previous firm had cultivated and left his former coworkers feeling like he had abandoned the mothership and exhibited disloyalty. There were not many well-wishers, and a lot of disappointment, particularly about the fact that he had been planning his exit for weeks and left suddenly without confiding in anyone. The rules in the broker-dealer arena are very established, and when you leave, abiding by those rules is critical; talking to anyone about your departure could prove fatal.

Loose lips sink more than ships; they can sink careers. As much as you might want to share your exciting news with others, keep your plans for departure as close to the vest as possible. The fewer people who know, the fewer who can accidentally pass it along. Sharing your plans with wholesalers can be particularly tragic as they pedal in information. If the mothership learns of your plans, they will not hesitate to cut you at the knees.

Carmine had a personal experience with this issue. He was best friends with the company's managing partner and thought he owed his buddy a heads-up out of respect. Carmine took a massive risk in sharing his news prior to his departure. The conversation turned contentious and ended the friendship, but it could have been much worse. Much of what you hear from former coworkers may be envy.

Both of us heard from colleagues who rationalized their continued servitude half-heartedly. They built narratives for themselves that justified all their practices, because of the kowtowing to corporate gods and the immense pressure they were under. They were miserable but lacked the initiative or the self-confidence to break up with this abusive partner. This cognitive dissonance is a natural response to a threatening situation, and it takes real initiative to overcome. Some of them did—and have since pursued independence.

Part of the strategy to move past the doubts is to remember why you're disrupting a career that has delivered good pay, amazing benefits, and outrageous perks. What is the impetus for trading that in, knowing that the transition may be profoundly challenging?

Carmine had the answer brought home to him one day at the new firm when he was chatting with an advisor from the old firm who was considering joining forces. The conversation was light and cheerful; the friend was upbeat and deeply curious with a million questions about what he could expect if he made the move. The answers about freedom, independence, relationships with clients, being a fiduciary, and working ethically had him visibly excited.

And then he looked at his watch.

Suddenly his shoulders slumped, his demeanor soured, and his face darkened. He was falling behind on writing insurance policies, he explained, and needed to go sell something. He went from the optimism of a discussion about freedom and ethical purity to thoughts of servitude and ethical compromise. He dreaded what he had to do next, both for himself and for his clients, but when your livelihood is threatened, one tends to focus on self-preservation. He was torn between the need to act honorably and in his customers' best interests and the need to feed his family and was depressed by the knowledge that he was about to choose the morally dubious option. He went from Cloud 9 to 6 feet under in a matter of seconds.

(He did eventually make the leap to join Carmine's firm—and he's killing it!)

And we never do. That's why we put ourselves through all the toil and trouble to unravel the corporate noose.

Key Lessons Learned

No matter how you leave, planning is critical. Having passed through the gauntlet, we have learned some key lessons about what you need prior to departure.

GET YOUR PERSONAL FINANCES IN ORDER!

It would be wise to have six months of cash flow in the bank before you leave in case you don't earn anything at the beginning. This is worst-case planning, and you probably won't need it, but the more prepared you are, the better. It will also allow you to make decisions that benefit your long-term prospects without jeopardizing your immediate financial situation. This may involve putting your family on an austerity plan for a while and tempering their expectations for vacations and other luxuries for a year or two. It's important that your wife and children understand the sacrifices they might have to make in the short term and the payoff in the long term.

KNOW YOUR EMPLOYMENT CONTRACT

Keeping in mind that we are not lawyers, and do not play ones on TV, and therefore cannot and are not offering legal advice, here is what we discovered was necessary with respect to the employment contract: have an attorney review your employment agreement so that you know in advance your rights and responsibilities pre- and post-resignation. It is imperative that you seek expert review and not rely on others' experiences because every firm is different and has its own requirements. Some firms have proprietary information that you are legally barred from taking. You don't want to give your bitter jilted lover justifiable means for a lawsuit.

STAY OFF EMAIL

This is so critical. Do nothing pertaining to the transition over company email. It's theirs and they own everything on the platform. Owning all your conversations and preventing you from accessing them is a double-win for them and a double-loss for you. They will keep you from seeing important information about the transition and have a comprehensive catalog of your planning. This is like finding your enemy's battle plan during war.

STAY OFF TEXT MESSAGES!

It is not likely that your text messages could be used against you, but it's possible. It's best to pick up the phone when communicating with anyone about your transition. Regulations prohibit texting about business via a nonmonitored and archived platform, so don't do it.

DON'T RUN YOUR MOUTH

As we mentioned before, you may feel inspired, or even obliged, to share your exciting news with that one friend in the office who you know will never tell anyone. Except, if you can't zip your lips, what makes you think they can? Keep the circle as tight as possible or risk your secret becoming public. We've seen people planning their departure getting summarily fired before they were ready to leave because management got wind of their plans. The rules around disengaging from a broker are not stacked in your favor.

In one case, we talked to two advisors preparing their escape who were posturing and talking like Rambo to everyone within earshot. At the time they were even bragging about getting sued. It was a big red flag for us because we knew what a big bag of hurt could come down on them if the wrong people heard it—or even if they didn't.

Leaving comes with consequences even in the best of circumstances, so be humble, leave quietly, and keep your head down so the bullets that start flying don't hit you in the noggin. For the big financial services firms, all's fair in love and advisors going independent. Don't give them a reason to make an example out of you.

CONFIRM THAT YOU'LL BE ABLE TO KEEP YOUR SOFTWARE LICENSE

There are very strict rules about who owns what client data. Lots of lawsuits have battled this one out. So, make sure you do your research and understand fully who owns what. This can vary by state and region of the country tied to appeals courts, so understand your state-specific requirements. Generally, accept that client data is not your data. The quickest way to end up on the wrong side of transition is to take something that is not legally yours. In most cases, you will not be able to maintain your software, data, etc. You will need to assume that you will be rebuilding everything from scratch. Assuming otherwise would be problematic.

IT'S NOT YOUR DATA

If we weren't clear enough earlier, it is not your data; take nothing other than what you are legally allowed. Know whether your firm is a "protocol" firm or not. If it is protocol, then follow the rules. If it's a non-protocol firm, then what you can take is extremely limited. Non-protocol transitions are particularly tricky. Having a team around you who understands the art of threading the transitions needle will prove invaluable.

HIRE AN ATTORNEY

You might think "you got this," but overconfidence in this game is a mistake. When hiring an attorney to guide you, select one who knows the former firm's attorneys because professional courtesy can lubricate the process and make your life easier and less emotionally fraught. Consider submitting your resignation on the attorney's letterhead so that the firm knows that you're loaded for battle and won't be easy to squash. The goal here is to dissuade the lawsuit.

It's important to leave quietly with humility. Did we mention humility? You don't want to give them any reason to sue you, which they will do as a warning to other advisors, even if they have no case. Sometimes winning only takes filing a lawsuit. The biggest victory in a lawsuit is to avoid one altogether. Lawsuits can cost hundreds of thousands of dollars only to settle. Cure yourself of an Erin Brockovich win, and just move on with your life.

CONSIDER THE WORST-CASE SCENARIO

And be prepared for it to occur. That way the only surprise is if it doesn't come to pass. Carmine knew his former firm could file a FINRA action against him, and they were happy to oblige. Not all FINRA actions are legitimate, and that doesn't mean they don't get filed. If you're busy dealing with legal troubles, guess what you're not doing, serving clients.

Carmine's troubles ate up fourteen months of his time and required significant legal fees to defend. It could have broken Carmine and sandbagged his firm. Being prepared and determining in advance where he would find his "break glass" money helped him withstand the blow emotionally, fight back with resources, and carry on during those fourteen months with the important task of building his new firm.

Also understand that lawsuits can be very emotionally taxing. It helps to frame them as just another business process. Try to step away from the emotion of it all and just work through the process.

DON'T BE A JERK

Indulging in disparagement is counterproductive. Maintaining a neutral or positive demeanor in all communications is key to avoiding unnecessary conflicts and preserving relationships. For instance, Carmine's resignation letter, despite his inner turmoil, consisted of three sentences expressing gratitude to the company for the opportunities provided. This written record serves as evidence of his integrity, demonstrating that he acted with grace until the end and beyond. Remember every word spoken and written and action taken will be scrutinized for at least a year. While it may seem overly cautious, maintaining this mindset is advisable before, during, and after any transition.

Don't Take It Personally

Don't assume anyone will throw rose petals at you for your brilliant and courageous business decision. Assume instead that you will suffer the slings and arrows of outraged business associates and clients who deep down may be envious that you are creating your own good fortune when they lack the fortitude to do the same. Be mindful, people generally dislike change, and by transitioning to independence, you are thrusting change on a lot of people. Low expectations will insulate you from disappointment and allow you to be pleasantly surprised if anyone offers good tidings.

Breaking away from a big firm and going independent is as much an emotional journey as a business transition, and emotions can often serve as a more formidable barrier than dollars and cents. Keep in mind that your previous employer and the leadership who runs the company will have to deploy a negative narrative about you to maintain their army of cogs. See it for what it is and rise above it emotionally.

MAKE SURE YOU'RE FULLY PREPARED

Being 80 percent prepared means you're 20 percent vulnerable, and that could lead to disaster. You will want to check off all these boxes in advance; otherwise, you could find that your move is even more challenging than it needs to be. Now that you have fully prepared for the big break and your future as an independent advisor, talk to your lawyer about what you can and can't say to your clients. This is one of the most important strategies you'll discover on your way to independence. It's worth repeating, the rules vary by state and circumstance.

CHAPTER 6

MESSAGING

You are in danger of living a life so comfortable and soft, that you will die without ever realizing your true potential.

—DAVID GOGGINS

We have a friend who handled the communications for a nonprofit organization. Much of his work involved developing branding and messaging for the internal team, meaning he dealt with internal customers and deadlines. He also had the following sign above his desk to deter emergency requests:

"Lack of planning on your part does not constitute an emergency on my part."

A lack of planning breeds poor results, whether you're a nonprofit communication department or, well, anything else. How many times have you told a client about their retirement that failing to plan is planning to fail? The more important the subject of the required plan, the more critical it is to have and follow it. That brings us to the immediate aftermath of your resignation from the mothership.

In the spirit of Dan Sullivan, the business author who penned the iconic business book *Who, Not How: The Formula to Achieve Bigger Goals through Accelerating Teamwork*, we are going to focus the next section of the chapter on helping you find the right people to put you on the path to success. We are not going to tell you how to make the transition. We are not lawyers—we don't even play lawyers on TV—so we are not offering you legal or any other advice here except to recruit into your transition the people who can grease the skids to success, reduce your agita, and find you the best parking spot. Or any two of those three.

As his book's title indicates, Sullivan deftly reorients readers away from focusing on how to get things done because that often puts the wrong people in the position of solving a problem; they are ill-equipped to solve. It also creates a micromanaging situation where the founder or CEO is pulling on their overalls and peering beneath the hood when they should focus their energies on the elements of the job; they know best and leave the trained mechanics to handle the problem. Instead of asking, "How do I do this?" he recommends you ask, "Who can help me achieve this?" That leverages the time and expertise of the right proper skill set for each issue.

Each transition situation is different. We hail from California and New Jersey, very different states with diverse laws. For example, in Carmine's state, it is against the law for any municipality not to sport at least one authentic Italian restaurant. Whereas where Daren lives, it is mandatory to hug a tree whose trunk exceeds 6 feet in circumference when passing it. (These may not be actual laws. As we say, we're not lawyers. But we can indeed say that defying these customs is socially unacceptable.)

Moreover, we left very different firms—one a life insurance company and the other a large brokerage—with different contractual languages about separation. Neither lovingly encouraged us to sprout our baby bird wings and fly away from the nest like a proud sparrow momma, but we faced different legal hurdles and compliance issues. It would be impossible to make global statements about what any single transition should look like. The only universal is to get the right people in your corner, so we offer you the right people.

From the get-go, we should mention that it may not be necessary to "find" the right people if you're bolting-onto an independent firm. Your new company may have people on board or the blueprint already written for your transition.

Between us, we have extracted several dozen Investment Advisor Representatives (IARs) from their big company gilded cages and have all the tools in hand for a transitioning advisor. We offer transition support advisors and help new advisors prepare to succeed financially and psychologically. But many firms do not or do so anemically. Or if you're opening your own firm, you won't have those resources and thus will need a transition team.

Why can't you do it yourself? Here's how we think: If you wanted to build a house, you could, eventually. It would be costly, painful, and interminable. Still, after many false starts, inspection failures, teardowns and rebuilds, unexpected costs, mistakes, and frustrations, you might learn enough to assemble something resembling a house. The water would stay where you want it, and many of the walls would approach perpendicularity—if you don't look too closely. The floors might squeak, but they would probably hold. But if you don't plan ever to build another house, what good are all the painful lessons you have learned constructing this house? You will never be able to apply for them.

Instead, you hire people who do this for a living and have already navigated around the potholes, absorbed the painful lessons, and developed strategies that avoid the worst issues. Bringing in a contractor and subcontractors to do it right, on time, and on budget will allow you to live happily ever after, or at least until your children reach their teen years.

THE PEOPLE YOU WILL ABSOLUTELY NEED TO SUCCEED

Keep in mind if you are bolting-on to a firm, many of these critical relationships will already be in place.

- *Relationship Consultant with Your Custodian:* Having an inside track on how to effectively work with your custodian(s) is very important. This is best achieved by fostering a relationship with your custodial representative(s).
- *Compliance Attorney/Consultant:* This is an absolute necessity. Trying to run a business without this person is a foolproof recipe for disaster. Interview this person carefully as they are all different.
- *Transition Consultant:* There is a tempo to transitioning effectively to becoming an independent advisor. In addition, there is a ton of data that needs to be managed when transitioning, and this person can help with that.
- *Transition Support Team:* These are the real worker bees of the transition. Having a great team to follow up on all the details will be invaluable.
- *Business Coach:* Not all advisors use coaches, but they should. If you're not investing 10 percent of your revenue into growing yourself as a person, advisor, and leader, you're selling yourself short. This is a mental game, and a good coach can help keep your game on point.

First, hire a lawyer or a transition coach as part of your departure plan. Have the lawyer review your employment contract and state statutes, and recommend a plan of action. Preferably, you use a lawyer who knows your state employment laws and FINRA rules. Most firms have contract language limiting when you can contact your clients. Some consultants and lawyers specialize by firm and by state. A guy in Arizona bills himself as the Schwab Killer, while another specializes in transitions from Edward Jones—and so on. (This is not an endorsement of any lawyer or individual transition coach; we're simply giving you an idea of the playing field.)

Our lawyers drew up our letter of resignation on their letterhead so that the firm knew we meant business and had done our homework before leaving. Again, the goal here is to dissuade any legal action. They knew we had stocked up on the necessary shark repellent and would be formidable opponents if they attempted to interfere with our departure. (Carmine's did regardless, to the regret of everyone but the lawyers.)

We recommend having a business coach who can help you navigate your swirl of emotions during the transition. World-class athletes and world-class advisors always have a coach. If you want to play at this level, so should you. There will be many during this process, and many will only interfere with your ability to withstand the pressures if you deal with them constructively. As noted, Daren runs, and Carmine meditates to let off the steam, but we both have coaches to help us let go of the negativity and focus on the positivity. (At least I'm not a Jets fan, thinks Daren. At least my team didn't move to Las Vegas, thinks Carmine.)

Carmine's attorney prepared him for all the potential issues that could follow his separation, and they all came to fruition. In that sense, he was like a meteorologist: he could predict the weather but couldn't stop the rain. The transition consultant taught Daren the process of determining what to include and what to avoid when building his messaging. So those are the who's—a lawyer/transition advisor and a business coach. It doesn't hurt to have a supportive spouse and a spoonful of self-confidence, too, but the strength you derive from them is only helpful if you know what you're doing.

One more note about preparing yourself mentally: There might never be a more helpful time for you to have an established exercise routine to assist you in releasing some of the stress. Carmine and Daren are both avid runners and spend time in the gym almost daily. In addition, we both had some preestablished meditation practice to help with those moments we found emotionally challenging.

So, now we have not provided you with any legal advice whatsoever but simply encouraged you, in a very nonlegal way, avoiding even a morsel of liability for your decisions, to hire the people who can guide you through your very individual circumstances that we in no way claim to understand (happy, legal department?). Let's follow Daren's transition consultant and head to the next step: the messaging.

MESSAGING TO STAKEHOLDERS

We both spent the entire weekend announcing that we had started our respective firms. We had hundreds of clients remaining at the firm from which we departed, most of whom did one or two transactions with us. Our interactions were transactional, not relational, and given the size of our portfolio of clients, there was no way we could provide them with the level of service they deserved and that we considered minimally adequate. For the most part, we chose not to announce to these people; if we did, they were not of high priority. We don't mean to be crass, but we understand that a single financial advisor cannot deliver high-quality, bespoke services and advice to six hundred customers.

WHAT DO YOU SAY TO CLIENTS?

Well, this topic is where the legal department does get involved. You are likely legally proscribed, prohibited, banned, restricted, and forbidden (have we made ourselves clear?) to announce anything *other* than the following: *you are excited to announce that you are leaving your old firm to start your own, to deepen your relationship with customers and change the customer experience.*

Period.

Again, what you can and cannot say is very state dependent. So, check with your lawyer first.

You are not permitted to solicit clients for the new firm. That will stir the legal demons and embroil you in a witches' brew of trouble that could invalidate your new firm. You must adhere without a jot or title of variance to your employment contract, which almost certainly prohibits (and all those synonyms) you from soliciting business from the firm's existing customers. That includes your best friend, your cousin (Vito in Carmine's case; Tree Plumbtree in Daren's; yes, Daren knows a guy by that name), and your sweet mother, who gave you life and then sacrificed for her welfare and never asked for anything in return.

A lawyer told us: "In connection with contacting clients, you are calling to announce your new affiliation only. You won't ask clients to move with you as you are not allowed to solicit clients under your agreement with [the company]. However, two sentences … will be helpful to narrow the focus of the client to the issue of choice."

> The two sentences are: "This is a service industry. You get to choose the advisor you work with."

Each employment contract is different, so be mindful of your statute of limitations on contacting clients.

We're not your lawyer—you need one, but he won't be us—so we're not going to get into the weeds much more here, and we certainly don't suggest you take any advice from us on legal topics. We want to offer this bit of nuance: while you may not solicit for a year after you leave, you may answer questions. Should a client inquire about whether and how they might follow you, with whom they have developed a relationship, rather than the faceless corporation into whose maw they will shortly be engulfed, that doesn't necessarily constitute a solicitation. Your clients think, "My financial advisor is Daren, or Carmine, or [your name here]," not "My financial advisor is Company X."

We remind you of this for two reasons. First, feeling optimistic about what you're doing is emotionally healthy. You will feel comfortable rather than anxious and fearful about your announcements. Second, people want to be a part of a vision and be led by others; that leader might as well be you. Share the vision, tell the story, and expand their horizons and the story of a better tomorrow.

Each of us wrote a script in advance, but we didn't read them word for word because reading a script can sound stilted and canned, the opposite of the feeling you want to create. You want the conversation to be friendly and natural. These are people with whom you have a relationship, after all. The script was talking points on steroids. Before we called, we considered all the possible questions clients might ask and prepared appropriate responses. The script's purpose was to create one consistent set of messages for all the advisors doing the outbound calling that would steer us away from tripping over our tongues under duress, or worse, stepping on the third rail of solicitation.

Your message, no matter the finer details of your situation, will likely sound the same as ours. You will sketch out your vision for the future, assuring the listener that you are embarking on a new path that will lead to superior service and more investment options and eliminate conflicts of interest. Like us, you can explain what a fiduciary is and how you will always work in your client's best interests.

That covers the script. You might have noticed what was not in our script and cannot be in yours:

- anything about your former employer

- anything about your dissatisfaction with them

- anything about the way they treated you

- any unethical demands they made

- any of the distorting incentives they offered

You will not explain to your clients the inside baseball details of the financial advisory industry and the plush junkets their continued patronage afforded you. Your message is entirely positive, forward-looking, and reflective of your vision of the future. It is focused on them and their financial well-being because the human spirit loves to be involved with a vision for something positive. You want your clients to feel like this is natural and good because they are about to face a hurricane of negativity—from the company you just left. Expect your former employer and her minions to do whatever they can to undermine you, your credibility, and your integrity. That's where the positive attitude and psychological hardiness come in.

If there is one piece of advice we can give you, it's to be positive and share your vision for a better future. People want to be a part of success; let them bring them into the vision for the future.

LET'S GET TACTICAL

That brings us to the message. You have planned your exit, consulted lawyers, submitted your resignation, dotted your "I's," and crossed your "T's." Now, you are ready to make your big announcement to your clients. You do that like you did everything else—by having a plan. Having a "go" binder is a way to take a lot of the emotion of transition away; when the time comes, you execute.

The following is a punch list of items that could be in your "go" binder:

• *Client Information:* Client confidentiality is critical; only capture the information you're ethically and legally permitted to possess regarding your clients, safeguarding their privacy and trust.

• *Centers of Influence (COIs):* The COIs you worked hard to establish should be on the top of your list. If you have shared clients, many of your clients will contact these COIs when they find out you have resigned to launch your own firm.

• *Communication Plan:* An orderly transition announcement list delineates the cadence at which you intend to inform stakeholders, ensuring a smooth and coordinated communication process during organizational transitions.

• *Scripts:* Scripts delineate permissible and prohibited language, guiding communication to adhere to legal, ethical, or professional standards in various contexts. Practice these before transitioning. Make them your words.

• *Questions and Answers:* A compiled list of anticipated questions with structured responses offers preparedness for expected inquiries, facilitating effective communication and mitigating uncertainties during interactions.

In our case, clients had questions, but they had more than that; they were excited about our message, which brought referrals! They were so energized by this new advisor-client arrangement that they thought of friends and associates who would also benefit from it and sent them our way. We received more introductions to potential new clients than we ever had prior. If clients were excited, professionals in related fields were thrilled. The CPAs, attorneys, and others who already understood what being a fiduciary is all about were most enthusiastic about our switch.

They did something even more remarkable: they demonstrated an extraordinary level of confidence by entrusting us with additional assets, seemingly indicating their readiness to fully commit to our partnership. In fact, because of this influx of new assets, despite having yet to take on a single new client for five months after securing his book of business, Carmine said he had his best year ever.

Those "why" conversations struck a chord with our clients that we didn't fully understand existed. Believe it or not, many of your clients understand the conflicts of interest you operate under. They stay with you because they like you. When you leave, we often hear they are relieved to no longer question whether you work in their best interests.

The more conversations we had, the more positive feedback we heard, the more it reinforced our decision, and the less anxiety we had about each subsequent conversation. We don't want to sugarcoat it: it was a brutal, emotionally draining endeavor. We took on a colossal challenge with plenty of ups and downs, and we learned a lot—including who our real friends were. But our clients were the best part of the process. Not long into the process, we began looking forward to each conversation as an opportunity to reconnect with the people whose futures we had been helping to shape. The conversations with clients were a ray of hope in the maelstrom of our lives. Years later, the glow from the very first moments of launching our new business have not worn off because we are doing right by clients who honor us with their business.

There will be a serendipitous side effect of this activity, writing a script and repeatedly engaging in this same discussion, each one a little different depending upon your conversation partner and the questions they ask: it will reinforce how you feel. Dozens, even hundreds of times, you will explain to others and remind yourself why it was imperative that you unlocked your golden handcuffs and escaped for a more promising and ethically defensible future. While caught in a whirlwind of emotions and uncertainty, your clients will reinforce your decision with their enthusiastic endorsement and support, or at least with their indifferent acquiescence, a measure of support. Clients who respond to your meticulously prepared messaging with a "yeah, whatever" are essentially demonstrating unqualified trust and deferring to your judgment.

Keep in mind: expect some surprises. Some people you are confident will stay with you will not—some people who you think won't, will. The mantra "some will, some won't, who cares, who's next" will be important throughout this process. Just keep going.

This concept is not conjecture; we experienced this ourselves. Our psychological state at the outset of the change was generous and sub-optimal until we began talking to clients. The conversations restored our faith in what we were doing, both because our message felt right and sounded true in our ears and because the conversations reminded us about how relationship based our work is. These conversations with people whose lives intertwined in ours, whose families we know, and whose welfare we care about and have sworn to promote—at least in the financial and, to some degree, psychological realms—buoyed our spirits and bolstered our self-confidence.

When the announcements began, we needed to put on a happy face and exude confidence to our clients. We were in "fake it 'til you make it" mode. However, after just a handful of meaningful discussions, the need for pretense vanished. We were genuinely exhilarated. This moment reinforced our dedication to weathering the immediate challenges, fully aware that more obstacles lay ahead on our journey. It solidified our commitment to persevere through the short-term pain, of which there was plenty more to come.

Our confidence was bolstered further by conversations with people in the know, in the industry or on the periphery, and with those COIs—the influential people we engage to help grow our businesses and whose businesses we refer individuals to. We are not the only professionals who rely on COIs to refer customers—real estate agents, healthcare advocates, estate planning attorneys, and consultants of all types also secure many of their clients through related professionals.

For financial advisors, those COIs include accountants, attorneys, personal lenders, trust underwriters, benefits specialists, mortgage professionals, marriage counselors, and more. All successful financial advisors dance to this tune because a single partner can account for dozens of new clients. These mutually beneficial relationships often grow beyond just business; they are personally and professionally fulfilling, satisfying, and enriching.

PRIORITIZE YOUR CENTERS OF INFLUENCE

At this fraught juncture in the transition, we dreaded our conversations with our COIs. After all, we had worked with them under one set of conditions and were now calling to announce we were altering the unwritten agreement. These were generally knowledgeable people in our field who would not be easily swayed; we expected that selling our new arrangement would require more effort than it did with semi-engaged clients who trusted our judgment. These people had relied on us, and suddenly, we informed them that we were leaving our firm and striking out on our own. They would want to know what we had done wrong, why we had been let go, and what rule or law we had broken. And if our responses were unsatisfactory, we could lose not just one influential client but a funnel of new clients for the rest of our careers. There was a lot at stake with each of the COI conversations, so we were apprehensive about their tone.

To our surprise, there was nothing to worry about; they were the most straightforward. They weren't the shortest but the most natural.

Our COIs were so supportive that they dismissed any concerns or objections. Most said something like, "It's about time" or "Of course you left." They were familiar with the conflicts of interest inherent in working for a big firm demanding sales of proprietary products. Several of them wondered how we had managed to hold out for so long. Most of them knew financial advisors who had taken the same step before and knew that life as a fiduciary was both more satisfying for the advisor and made for better referrals.

They were aware of our internal struggles with the ethical dilemmas confronting us; in fact, several of them told us that they liked referring to us precisely because we were resistant to the hard sell, that they could count on us to operate in the best interest of their clients. After all, it would reflect poorly on them if they referred someone to us who was dissatisfied with our service. No matter how friendly we are with our COIs, no matter how much the personal relationship enters it, this is ultimately a matter of business. No one in any profession can continue to refer clients to an unreliable COI partner.

So, did we lose COIs? We *gained* additional ones. More professionals in tangential disciplines wanted to join forces with us once we became fiduciaries. People get it. It's like when you date someone none of your friends like, but they are all too scared to tell you. When you break up with the disliked individual, all your friends say, "It's about time."

Conversations with potential new clients began sooner than either of us expected in either of our situations because our COIs grew and widened. It hadn't occurred to us that COIs are not only great for referring clients, but they can also refer to other COIs, and that's precisely what happened when we moved to a fiduciary model.

Our pivot reminded our old COIs, friends, and informal business partners that there were others with whom they could connect us and that this would be a great time to do it. "You should talk to my friend Daren. He's a great guy, and he just ditched the big firm to open his own shop as an independent financial advisor. That means if you use him as your financial advisor, he works for you, not for the insurance company or financial services firm. He can choose the best investment for you among all the options, not just among the options his company sells" is what we imagine our COIs told their colleagues. This advocacy is partly responsible for our ability to grow our book of business even in that tumultuous first year of the new operation.

It's difficult to overstate the importance of the COIs to our business and the immense relief we felt when they were not only on board with our decision to strike out on our own but also actively encouraging it. We have been carving time out to meet for coffee or a meal, entertain at ball games and concerts, and share information with these people.

We're scratching each other's backs professionally and developing relationships. We had been sharing a piece of our vision with them prior to the breakaway, but afterward, we took the time to reconnect with each of them and paint the complete picture for them. Now that we have nothing to hide, the conversation is a lot smoother, not that we weren't always being honest. We always tell the truth and nothing but the truth but perhaps not the whole truth. Now, we would be perfectly comfortable putting one hand on a Bible and swearing to do all three.

One of the most satisfying side effects of all this was something we did not do. For the first time in our careers, we were no longer required to walk our clients through the long, obtuse, arcane, lawyer-speak client disclosure form, acknowledging to our customers that we had an inherent conflict of interest. Both of us, independently, worked hard to minimize, if not eliminate, that conflict (otherwise, we might still be at the global conglomerate, cashing their checks and traveling on their junkets).

It's different, though, when you don't have to question your own motives constantly or limit your client to just the options available when you know there might be better ones in the marketplace. Going independent, eliminating conflicts of interest, and no longer having to read our clients' disclosure forms is a bit like having knee surgery and no longer enduring pain when you walk. By eliminating the necessity of acknowledging potential conflicts, you forget quickly how happy you are to avoid this emotionally corrosive procedure unless you remind yourself every once in a while about the pain you aren't feeling. Writing a book is an effective way to shake the memories loose, but it comes with plenty of its own agony, particularly if you're as naturally gifted at writing as you are at, say, pole vaulting.

Consider what Carmine had to tell his clients when he advised them to purchase life insurance manufactured by his company. As we've said, there is nothing inherently wrong with this practice; in fact, these are quality products that might very well serve the best interests of the client. But when the company pressures advisors to sell more and more of these policies beyond the point where they are advisable, a conflict of interest is inevitable, even if no one acknowledges that it is the primary driver of this advice.

As a CERTIFIED FINANCIAL PLANNER™, Carmine was required to hand each potential client a "Conflict of Interest Disclosure Form" provided by the insurance company. Why? Because he was dipping his toe—and then his foot, ankle, and leg—into the muddy waters of conflict of interest.

Here is part of the Conflict of Interest form:

> I have what some might consider to be certain conflicts of interest when I make an investment recommendation to you: I recommend products that [our company] manufactures. I can only offer securities products approved by [our company]. The universe of products I have available for recommendation consists of proprietary products in the case of variable annuities and variable life products. [Our company] believes that this singular focus assures that I have a developed understanding and ability to explain our proprietary variable annuity and variable life products and the financial strength of the guarantees that [our company] offers. My compensation depends in part on the volume of sales of products [our company] and its subsidiaries manufacture. Sales of products [our company] manufactures, along with mutual funds it does not manufacture, determine my eligibility for retirement, medical, and life insurance benefits and to attend conferences with educational, development, and recognition components. Qualification to attend [our company]-sponsored educational, training, and development conferences is based on my total sales of investment and annuity products, life insurance [our company] manufactures, and long-term care insurance.

What a relief to know that we won't have to subject our clients to that again.

While you're sticking to the script and remaining positive about your new venture, the lords of the financial realm will be unencumbered by such quaint notions as propriety and sportsmanship. They do not like being crossed or allowing anyone to feel as if they have triumphed against them. They have yacht payments to make, bonuses to brag about at the country club, and thousands of remaining advisors whose heads they do not want filling with dreams of sugar plums and happy separations.

On the contrary, they plant seeds of fear in every employee's head and fertilize them at every opportunity, insinuating that anyone who leaves is guilty of treason, engaged in foul play, and will pay a hefty price for their heresy. Maintaining control of the great unwashed (even if they wear suits) is no different in a big corporate structure than it is in, say, the dictatorship of your choice—Russia, China, the NFL. The muckety-mucks do not suffer dissent or disloyalty gladly, and woe to those who attempt to speak truth to power.

We're guessing the next chapter will be a revelation for you. But you should know what to expect so that you can be prepared to deal with every possible scenario.

CHAPTER 7

WHAT TO EXPECT

We must walk consciously only part way toward our goal, and then leap in the dark to our success.

—HENRY DAVID THOREAU

Consider all that has transpired in your life and career to get you to this point. You joined the industry, learned your craft, built your book of business, developed relationships with clients, honed your techniques, and dedicated yourself to understanding the latest products, tax implications, and macroeconomic factors.

You collected your checks and enjoyed the junkets along the way, but you also began to see the dark side. You began sweating the details, worrying about keeping up with the sales requirements, and chafing over the ethical dilemmas involved in situations you found yourself in. You started questioning whether you were getting a fair share of the income you were generating and whether you were truly working in your customers' best interests.

Eventually the questions outnumbered the answers. You entered that Middle Earth stage where you weren't ready to leave but wondered whether your current arrangement was sustainable. Your blood pressure spiked; your sleeping hours dwindled. How long did that last—months? Years?

Significant life changes generally do not appear with the snap of fingers, like the asteroid crash that extinguished the dinosaurs and most other Earth species. So, if you've found yourself immersed in dissatisfaction for a year or two, take heart: transformation is a gradual journey.

Eventually, the ball crosses the goal line, and you are ready to act. Even then, you're merely in the research and development stage. You start sniffing around other advisors who have made the change and asking about the process. You begin researching the relevant financial arrangements. You realize just how many mental heuristics are involved in calculating how you get paid. You discover that payout ratios for financial services firms vary widely by firm and product type.

According to FinancialPlanning.com, 2019 payouts for mutual funds were as follows: Ameriprise Financial: 90–95 percent; AXA: 50–91 percent; Kestra Financial: 65–95 percent; MML Investor Securities: 40–83 percent; and SFA Partners: 90–92 percent. (The complete list is much longer; we just pulled five at semi-random across the alphabet.)[13]

You need to know the fees you will pay for all the administrative requirements. For example, consider the advisory administration fee if you're planning to manage your clients' assets yourself. Expect to pay ten to thirty basis points for billing, client statements, and performance reporting. There are countless other potential fees across various arrangements, all of which you must determine before severing ties with the corporate structure. While we could write chapters on this one point, we will save you the suffering. Simply put, having an excellent team to support you will help you navigate the options.

There is still much more to be done, even once the decision to fly north is made. First, decide whether to fly solo or bolt-on to an independent firm. Write the departure plan, build a "go" binder, save the cash, and prepare the family. Draft the client script and research the hardware and software you will need. Collect the necessary data to continue delivering exceptional service to clients. Hire a lawyer and write your resignation letter.

You've done all that and here you are. Prepare for takeoff in 3...2...1... Blast off!

Whew—you survived. We did and you will, too.

There was a movie in the 1970s called *The Candidate*. Robert Redford plays a charismatic young politician who agrees to wage a quixotic campaign for the governor against a popular incumbent to gain favor within his party for future opportunities and spread his idealistic messages. As the campaign ensues, the party handlers begin fine-tuning his speeches to widen his appeal, and the polling gap narrows. With the cynical spin doctors increasingly in control, the message becomes more generic, losing its idealism and gaining electoral support.

By the movie's end, Redford's character squeaks out a thrilling and unexpected electoral triumph, an outcome even he was unprepared for. During the victory party, he pulls aside his chief political handler and asks the question that brings down the curtain on the movie:

"What do we do now?"

That is the stage you have just entered.

THE ANNOUNCEMENTS WILL EXCITE, DEPRESS, AND CONFOUND YOU

You have endured the gauntlet of disengagement from the talons of fear, compromised values, and psychic pain. You have your script, and you make announcements. The fear of rejection quickly ebbs once you begin your conversations, particularly if you have emotionally prepared yourself to endure the agony of defeat and the thrill of victory. So, what do you do now?

First, you dispel all your expectations in advance. You will not keep all your friends or those you believe are your friends. One or two whom you are confident about share your feelings will express disappointment or outrage and accuse you of disloyalty to them personally. On the other hand, some colleagues will surprise you in the affirmative. You didn't give them credit for being open-minded, tolerant, or particularly supportive of you and your career. Still, they wish you the best, connecting you with people or offering ideas to help you progress. Your only expectation should be that the unexpected will occur. You don't really know who's coming with you until they are coming with you.

Here's what we both learned with our assumptions: you simply never know. We both ended up with more sizable assets under management, revenue, and profit than we expected, though we have learned that is not always the case. It was like taking a cross-country road trip in your car and estimating the time it would take. You might arrive at your destination earlier than anticipated despite encountering some unforeseen roadblocks in unlikely places like central Kansas and some unexpected smooth sailing like through a big city.

Another variable is the response from the firm you are leaving. Some companies have a battle plan at their elbow and plenty of experience grappling for every client. They enter DEFCON 5 and implement their tried-and-true plan, which can include whispers about your mental stability, aptitude as a financial advisor, or commitment to being a fiduciary, or it may focus on benign topics like their one hundred years of experience managing portfolios and assurances of improved performance. In either case, a strong counterattack presents a tremendous challenge.

On the contrary, a company that sees the futility of fighting back and has experienced only marginal success when trying to maintain clients may present a listless and token response (opt for that one if the choice presents itself!).

Daren's former firm had a well-oiled fighting machine and got on the phone immediately to intercede and frame the narrative. However, Carmine's ex-firm took three weeks to meander back into the fray; clients were set with their decision by then. In the end, it doesn't matter all that much; what matters is your relationship with your clients. The details of how and when you contact them matter, but relationships supersede logistics.

DON'T LET PERFECTION BE YOUR ENEMY

One mindset that will enable the path to emotional well-being during the initial days of transition is an adjunct to the idea of sidelining your expectations. Our motto when it comes to rebuilding your book of business: 100 percent is for losers.

Don't get us wrong; we would have loved to sing kumbaya around the campfire with all our pre-transition relationships. We both highly approve of everyone loving us. Bring on the adulation! Thank you, Denver! Oh, we're in Cleveland? Thank you, Cleveland! We would have been thrilled to see every customer lighting their phones for an encore and posting their undying love for us on social media as if we were Taylor Swift. (To be crystal clear, neither of us is Taylor Swift;

we're rarely confused with her in airports and at conventions. In the shower, however, you might confuse us with Bruce Springsteen.)

The problem with 100 percent is that it's not a good business decision. It's like those public opinion polls asking people if they support the death penalty for parking tickets or serving rat poison with school lunches. When they announce that the public overwhelmingly opposes both by a landslide, with 94 percent opposed and 6 percent in favor, you must wonder who those 6 percent nutcases are. We're not proposing that your clients are nutcases, but there will always be outliers. Aiming for unanimity is just dancing the tango with futility and a prescription for disappointment.

Aiming to capture that outlying 10 to 20 to 30 percent will distort the message for the bulk of your relationships who are only too happy to join you on this new journey. Stay off the 100 percent road and travel a path where you are more inclined to capture the largest number of your best relationships, knowing that there will be losses. When taking on a "best-interest" standard, exclusivity is your friend. Not everyone should be your client.

The average relationship retention rate is about 30–80 percent, depending on circumstances. Why?

You will discover countless interlocking relationships preventing people from migrating over with you. We experienced numerous circumstances: some people had a personal affiliation with the original firm, like a sister who works in their legal department. Others kept a portion of their portfolio with us and the rest with someone else. When we announced our departure, they took the path of least resistance and left all their holdings with the other folks.

Daren took on a noteworthy new client shortly before leaving his previous employer. During their original discussions, she demanded to know how long he planned to remain with the firm, forcing him to tap dance around the issue. By law, the industry prohibits financial advisors from revealing to clients if they plan to leave their current firm. This rule is another example of how big firms create a conflict between their workforce and clients. Daren would have been transparent with her if that hadn't put him in legal jeopardy; in this case, being transparent could be interpreted as "selling away."

She was furious when he announced his departure, insisting that Daren had misled her. Daren considered not taking on any new clients for some time prior to departing, but if production dropped, that would have drawn additional unwanted scrutiny. It's a no-win situation. Rather than blaming the firm or the industry, this individual blamed Daren, the messenger, who, in effect, devised the rules related to the transparency, and she had to be chalked up as a loss. Transition is imperfect, and you will have these bumps along the way. The key is to keep going. Winston Churchill is often credited with saying, "If you're going through hell, keep going."[14]

When we said we wanted to be valued, that's only partly true. In hindsight, we realized that while adulation would have been welcome, neither of us genuinely desired to maintain every relationship at all costs, and it's likely that you shouldn't either. When growing a business, only some relationships that were once a great fit are still a great fit. The ever-evolving ideal client dilemma is one that many struggle with within the industry. Transitioning to a new firm is an excellent opportunity to adjust one's ideal relationship base. Some of those left behind were merely transactional clients, people with whom we had had little or no ongoing contact. These are not high-value relationships or high-value prospects.

Moreover, recognizing that there are only 168 hours a week—and you must spend some of that time calling one another and mocking the taxes in California and the chemical plants in New Jersey—it is malpractice to keep three hundred clients and expect to deliver anything remotely close to adequate service to them. This unsustainable model is the preferred operating method for large financial services firms—they prioritize constant expansion—sell more, more, ever more. However, we value our relationships and, consequently, found it necessary to trim our client roster. This reality exemplifies that big firms are in the sales business, solidifying our desire to be in the relationship business.

While it may be tempting to maintain as many of your relationships as possible, some relationships are better suited for someone else, and you're better for it. Carmine had one client who liked him but just wanted to buy bonds. There was no argument for him to come along and pay an advisory fee. One relationship told Daren he just wanted his help executing transactions and didn't value the wealth management aspect of the relationship. We wished them Godspeed in both cases and moved on to better fits. You must be thoughtful and selective about those you agree to let join you, especially because now that you're a fiduciary, they can sue you when you mess up. If you bring everyone along, it is a sign that you must clarify your vision more precisely.

All that said, we were very successful in maintaining the relationships that we valued most.

HOW ABOUT YOUR COLLEAGUES? FUHGEDDABOUDIT!

That is the client side. Then there is the professional side. When you leave, you will leave all your colleagues in the company behind. If you work for a printing company, physician's practice, or a plumbing supply store and exit to forge your own path, leaving on good terms despite the new competition for customers is possible. There is an unspoken understanding that everyone is acting on their own ambitions, whether collecting the gold watch or moving on when the moment suits you.

Accountants who jump to the competitor in town, athletes who sign a contract with an opposing team, real estate agents who take their contacts to the rival company—all of them are understood to be doing what is best for them. Only in financial services is this somehow considered an unpardonable heresy. This is because rules have been designed by regulatory bodies, bought by the large brokers, to keep the COGS in seat.

The irony here is that in all the examples we offered, the departing worker would have a much *greater* affiliation with the big company than we had. They would be employees with a guaranteed paycheck, health insurance, and vacation time. They would have a desk at the company office and work alongside their colleagues there. Their loyalties, unlike ours, would be entirely to the company. Our loyalty was and always is to our company, with which we have an intimate relationship, as the owner. If you ask an Amazon, Exxon, or FedEx employee whom they work for, they will name Amazon, Exxon, or FedEx. If you ask a financial advisor, they might tell you the name of their firm or say they work for themselves. They might tell you they represent Global Insurance Conglomerate, Inc., but the local office has their name on it.

The point here is that we have looser bonds to Big Brother than almost any other profession, and yet, our decision to apply our trade elsewhere often creates bad blood, the kind not seen in other businesses. It's like an old joke about why the politics in academic departments is so vicious. The answer: because they don't matter.

You probably know what is coming: when the grapevine heated up and word got out about our new venture, the fallout was predictably mixed, which is to say far more negative than it should have been. After all, if you left your job as a physical therapist at Johns Hopkins for the same job at the Mayo Clinic, you would be shocked to hear a single discouraging word, much less a chorus of anger and bitterness. On the contrary, you might expect a goodbye party, parting gifts, and hosannas from your coworkers. Perhaps you don't think the analogy is exact, since you wouldn't take clients, but it's not too far off. In every other profession, people wish one another the best in their future endeavors. But because the big firms pepper their advisors with a steady stream of "us versus them" propaganda about loyalty, not all minds are ready to hear that there are cracks in the logic.

Be prepared for blowback, and for dismissing those who express anger, disappointment, betrayal, and frustration as projecting their own discontent with the circumstances rather than with you per se. Daren received multiple notes from colleagues stating their disappointment in him. One note he received from a mentor at his previous firm still echoes, "I am disappointed in you." The loss of friendships and colleagues will hurt, but stay focused on your true north. Know the why behind what you're doing. As the Bible teaches, "Forgive them, for they know not what they do" (Luke 23:34 KJV).

Once you leave, some of the people you consider your friends at the firm will give you reasons why they must stay. You become their mirror. That's okay; they will continue to operate as they do now, for good or ill, or will eventually join you in a transition they are currently unprepared to make. Give them their space because you have much bigger fish to fry. See the person, not the firm they work for, and rise above the propaganda they are fed.

Engaging with every displeased former colleague who feels personally insulted opens the door to a soap opera that you don't want to play a part in. It's like celebrities getting trolled on Twitter; they must learn to just let it go because responding to the trolls leads to descent into their subterranean world where the rats and cockroaches live. As the old saying goes, "Never get into a pissing match with a skunk." It is best to focus on your new journey and vision and cease communication with anyone from your old firm, as communication with previous colleagues could lead to a lawsuit. Additionally, anything you say could be pulled into legal proceedings. Your previous employer will use anything you say against you. By sharing much with friends, you could accidentally pull them into a lawsuit.

That isn't to say you should ignore your friends but differentiate between those who are important to you and who appear open to a discussion and those who are just spewing venom. Also remember that you need to protect your friends from being drawn into a deposition should your old employer elect to come after you. The best way to protect your friends is to avoid oversharing. We were shocked by the composition of some of our detractors. Some of our best friends in the business were disappointed in us, and some people we didn't credit were our biggest champions. We are convinced that their reaction said a lot more about them than about us.

It is important to remember that change is disruptive, and people have varying capacities for it and reactions to it. Again, expect the unexpected and nothing surprises or catches you off guard. You're rolling the dice with your business relationships when you break away, and while it makes sense to expect 6s, 7s, and 8s, occasionally, you roll boxcars or snake eyes. If at any point you feel emotionally spent by the drama, just step back and think in the long term.

CONSULT THOSE WHO HAVE WALKED IN YOUR SHOES

One of the things we did to prepare for our move was to survey advisors who had paved the way before us. In a way, we were requesting from them what we're accomplishing for you through this book: equipping you for a substantial shift in your professional journey that is bound to be both tactically and emotionally challenging, potentially leading to financial instability or, at the very least, a phase of uncertainty. We took their advice, and that made all the difference to us and has layered on our experience, which we hope will accrue to your benefit and many more traveling the same path. It seems dangerous to throw a bomb on fourth and one at your own 30-yard line, but less so if you know the opposing team is planning a safety blitz and your receivers will be one-on-one with their cornerbacks.

Departing from the parent company and venturing independently evoke apprehension in every business sector, whether within an advertising agency, an accounting firm, or a plumbing supply store. Even in the best of circumstances where the interpersonal issues are manageable, the laws are silent, and no employment contract presents barriers to departure, it is a leap off a cliff into the unknown. Being an entrepreneur is not for the weak-minded, no matter the field. Everyone who has ever started their own business can regale us with tales of woe and document a litany of stumbling blocks they had to overcome with grit, perseverance, and faith. They had to learn not just their trade but also how to market their service or product, manage an office, handle a payroll, lead employees, build a culture, select vendors, negotiate deals, and so on.

Throw into the bouillabaisse the bitter ingredients of ethical conflicts, war over clients, innuendos about your character and performance, and a counteroffensive from the former team to prevent the transference of customers, which significantly ups the ante, literally. There is a much greater down payment, or initial investment, not just financially but also psychically, to leaving a warehouse or insurance company than to starting a new construction company, an auto repair shop, or an ophthalmologist's office.

We asked those before us what we could do to make that first year as pain-free as possible. How could we knock down some speed bumps they had ridden over? We heard a lot of what you have read in this book. Many of the tips, large and small, that we have offered you owe their provenance to the thirty to forty independent advisors we conferred with before we went out on our own. We asked them about the worst thing that happened to them and how we might secure the shark repellent for that. We heard the stories and thought we could get through it.

And then, the worst thing happened to Carmine.

The company sued him when two other advisors determined their lot would be improved working with an independent firm. As we have mentioned, big businesses often engage in strangulation by litigation against small businesses. It doesn't matter whether the lawsuit is legitimate or who will ultimately prevail in a court case; what matters is the cost of litigation for the small firm. Often, even winning the case in court could be fatal because the legal fees would drown the enterprise. That is precisely what happened to Carmine, who settled to avoid escalating legal costs. Here is his perspective:

I wouldn't change a thing about it because I gained three important and positive benefits:

1. If I had taken the money I spent on this and went to every "self-help" seminar out there, it still would not have given me 10 percent of the mental toughness I gained.

2. If this large insurance company was so upset about me leaving and encouraging others to go as well, it confirmed that I was on the right track because they represent what I believe is wrong with our industry.

3. It built my credibility. I survived the worst-case scenario and thrived through it! I could have avoided the whole thing by not allowing the two other advisors to accompany me. That company coming after me was one of the best things that could have happened to me.

It's a small victory for me that my settlement didn't cover their costs, and over the next two years, I more than made up for it. I'm now much better off financially and my life is much better. Now when I go on vacation with my family, I am totally present for my wife and kids.

One last thing we asked our advisor friends: What was their biggest regret about making the move? Their answers were unanimous: that they should have done it sooner. Despite all the landmines, every one of them felt they had made the right move—so much so that they wondered what had taken them so long. All of them were happier as independent advisors than working for the big firms. They all felt they were delivering superior service to their clients. Sure, the first six months were a grind, but the struggle was noble and helped them build a more resilient practice.

Now, add us to the list. That would be our answer today. We both stewed over the question of whether, and then how, to leave for months. We lived in a perpetual state of bad emotional weather and ill wind. When we finally pulled the trigger, it was as rigorous a process as we expected. And it didn't take long for the skies to clear and sunshine to pour into our lives.

So, have you made your decision? Can you do this now that you know more about what to expect? If so, here are some final pieces of advice because—take it from us—the path you'll be taking and the decisions you'll be making will be based on emotion more than anything else, even money.

IT GETS BETTER, FAST

In the immediate aftermath of your break from the mothership, there will be a whirlwind of activity. Kiss your partner and kids' goodbye for the next month, and bring a toothbrush and change of clothes to the office. With all there is to overcome, it's a sprint to the starting line. Consider this arithmetic: you will work twenty-five hours—eight days a week, ten times as hard as before, for a total work output of 431.6 Blonskinos. (We just made up that unit of measurement but are quite pleased with it. One Blonskino equals the amount of work you would ordinarily do in each period.)

In that month, you will open an office, purchase computers and software, integrate all your systems, make your announcement calls, invite new clients to your new firm, hire staff, meet with everyone you can, engage in 192 phone calls with your lawyer, and much more. It's a mad, emotional rush to survive in those first thirty days—and it's totally unsustainable.

During this time, of course, you will need the support of your partner, if that's applicable because if they aren't wrangling the kids while you're away, no one is. You'll need the forbearance of your friends and other family members, whose texts and phone calls will go unanswered. You might as well record a voicemail saying, "If you're a friend, family member, or my significant other, and you don't have an account with me, I can't talk to you this month. I'll try to fit you in next month."

Things do slow down over the next sixty days because they must. No one can run full speed indefinitely. There are still quadrillions of things to do, but they're not all a top priority anymore. You have switched from dead sprint to marathon mode. Settle into a rhythm, breathe, and resume human interaction with those small people with early bedtimes who have moved into your home.

And now here's some excellent news.

After ninety days, the urgency is gone, and you've resumed life's normal pace. In fact, at this same spot on our journeys, independently (indeed, we didn't even know each other yet) and on opposite sides of the country, we both did the same thing: we took time off. We did it in different ways—Carmine took a vacation with his wife, and Daren chilled at home—but we got away and recharged in both cases. It was evident that we had crossed the Rubicon in better shape than we had imagined and had begun the process of operating successful businesses.

One thing does change, though: you suddenly have so much more time for prospecting, networking, and client contact. You've shifted from retention mode to growth mode like before. Why? It now strikes you with clarity how excessively you had been inundated with meaningless paperwork tailored to appease brokerage compliance gods to protect the brokerage from you—that's right, you—when regulators come knocking brokerages are careful to lay the footwork, so that if the music stops, they can point the finger at you. If you listened to nothing else, we have said, ponder on that one.

Now, the need for initiative has replaced the need for permission—in triplicate. You're no longer playing Twister with your conflicts of interest and documenting all the ways in which you did not break the law or company policy or all the ways you did fulfill company CYA requirements. You're simply acting in what you consider the best interest of your clients. The ethical tightrope and all the accompanying documentation are gone. Being a fiduciary is *freeing*.

Here's an example of the tight controls our former employers clamped on us. When Daren joined his previous firm, they agreed to allow him to continue doing leadership training on a limited basis, as he had done earlier in his career. Eight months into his employment, they revoked that agreement. There was nothing Daren could do about the bait and switch. They claimed they didn't want him to get distracted. More likely, the reasoning was more of a compliance issue. Now, we do whatever we think is good for business, such as leadership training, or whatever we think is simply good, like philanthropic activities.

We know you think this is all just more hyperbole, but you can't overestimate how much of your time at the big firm is consumed with business tracking paperwork to protect the brokerage from the broker rather than to serve clients. The brokerage's #1 priority is to avoid trouble, like a lawsuit, that might clog the profit-production machine. Once you break away, all the irrelevant minutia dissipates. In our shops, we do quarterly check-ins with our teams to keep them accountable; otherwise, we leave them alone to make good decisions.

That said, freedom can be dangerous. Freedom overload is real for those lacking the intrinsic discipline to reign themselves in, structure their time, and focus on productivity. Some advisors who go independent lose their business mindset because nothing extrinsic forces them to respect their business 8–5 every day. Daren knows one advisor who started working from home and allowed his personal life to bleed into his professional life. His wife tasked him with daytime kid management since he was home, blurring the lines between family and work and draining his time spent on the business. Not surprisingly, his business began dwindling. Don't get us wrong, families are by far our most important focus, but if you want to build and grow a business, nothing circumvents focused time working on the business.

We have no illusions that this book is not for every financial advisor; we're confident that two-thirds of the industry will have no use for it. Advisors who lack the innate desire to achieve won't be interested in leaving the nest. Advisors who love recognition, the leaderboard, the trophies, the perks, and those who need the security of the corporate womb, they're not going anywhere. They will follow the company rules, make a good living, collect their gold watch from Behemoth Conglomerate Inc., and retire happily.

If you're like us, you're the other third, driven to provide exceptional service to your clients, remain on the cutting edge of knowledge, grow your book strategically, and earn ever more for your increasing expertise; this is for you. Though the journey may be tough at the outset, the rewards will enrich your entire career ahead.

As a final thought, don't forget to enjoy the journey. The only truly precious commodity is time. The time you have on this Earth to make an impact and perhaps change it for the better. Should you choose the road to independence, remember to sit back and appreciate the moments. Your life will be full of people to talk to and things to do. Take a pause and be grateful.

The path to success is not easy, but the rewards of perseverance are immeasurable.

—ROY T. BENNETT

ABOUT THE AUTHORS

Daren Blonski, CFP®, is the cofounder and managing principal of Fermata Advisors/Sonoma Wealth Advisors. He is a learner, educator, and entrepreneur. With a master of arts in psychology from Sonoma State University, he is deeply connected to helping clients take their lives to the next level. His clients see him as a coach, operating in the realm of financial planning.

Working with clients across the life-stage spectrum, he focuses particularly on assisting entrepreneurs looking to soak up life. Coupling his experience with traditional markets, Daren specializes in helping clients who value Bitcoin and other cryptos to build diversified investment strategies.

A lifelong learner, Daren is a CERTIFIED FINANCIAL PLANNER™, an Accredited Investment Fiduciary™, a Certified Retirement Planner Specialist™, a Certified Exit Planning Advisor™, a Certified Retirement Planning Counselor™, an Accredited Asset Management Specialist™, a Smartvestor Pro™ with Dave Ramsey, and a Certified Digital Asset Advisor™ and has received his certificate in blockchain and digital assets from the Digital Assets Council of Financial Professionals. He is deeply committed to the pursuit of lifelong learning.

As a lifelong resident of Sonoma County, if there is a race to be run, a weight to be lifted, a mountain to be climbed, Daren is all in. He loves the outdoors, fishing, and Red Sox Baseball. He spends his spare time pursuing his physical and mental agility through various outdoor and physical health-related activities. With all this said, Daren's greatest joys are his three children: Brooklyn, Bryton, and Brady.

Carmine Corino, Certified Financial Planner™, is the visionary behind Cornerstone Planning Group, a national wealth management firm dedicated to empowering clients and advisors to craft secure futures. Departing from the corporate-constrained environment to establish an independent RIA, Carmine has steadfastly pursued an ethos of Impact and continues to enrich the lives of his clients and liberate other advisors from restrictive corporate settings. He champions collaboration and prioritizes personal development, regularly engaging with multiple business coaches and mastermind groups across the nation.

Apart from his professional pursuits, Carmine embodies the essence of a true fitness enthusiast. Whether he's pounding the pavement, swimming laps in the pool, or pushing weights in the gym, Carmine dedicates himself to physical fitness to enhance his capabilities as an advisor and enrich his roles as a husband, father, and individual. Above all, his utmost happiness comes from embarking on adventures around the world alongside his wife, Alexis, and their two children, Mia and CJ.

ENDNOTES

1   Malcolm Gladwell, *Blink: The Power of Thinking Without Thinking* (New York: Little, Brown and Company, 2005), 14.

2   Samantha Rosenthal, "31% of investors don't know how much they pay in investment fees, survey shows," CNBC, April 4, 2023, https://www.cnbc.com/2023/04/04/31percent-of-investors-dont-know-how-much-they-pay-in-investment-fees.html.

3   Ibid.

4   Bruce Kelly, "Which firms pay advisers the most?" Investment News, April 21, 2012, https://www.investmentnews.com/which-firms-pay-advisers-the-most-44667.

5   "DiSC® Styles," DiSCprofile.com, accessed March 14, 2024, https://www.discprofile.com/what-is-disc/disc-styles.

6   Ibid.

7   Ibid.

8   "Occupational employment and wages, May 2021: 13-2052 Personal Financial Advisors," U.S. Bureau of Labor Statistics, March 31, 2022, https://www.bls.gov/oes/current/oes132052.htm.

9   "2022 Evolution revolution: a profile of the investment adviser profession," Investment Adviser Association and National Regulatory

Services, 2022, https://higherlogicdownload.s3.amazonaws.com/INVESTMENTADVISER/aa03843e-7981-46b2-aa49-c572f2d-db7e8/UploadedImages/publications/Evolution_Revolution_2022.pdf.

10   Deloitte, "2017 Global mobile consumer survey: US edition," accessed March 15, 2024, https://www2.deloitte.com/us/en/pages/technology-media-and-telecommunications/articles/global-mobile-consumer-survey-us-edition.html.

11   Jonathan A. Obar and Anne Oeldorf-Hirsch, "The Biggest Lie on the Internet: Ignoring the Privacy Policies and Terms of Service Policies of Social Networking Services," *Information, Communication & Society* 23, no. 1 (2020): 128–147, https://doi.org/10.1080/1369118X.2018.1486870.

12   Antoine de Saint-Exupéry, *Terre des Hommes* (*Wind, Sand and Stars*), trans. Lewis Galantière (New York: Reynal & Hitchcock, 1939), 157.

13   Barbara A. Friedberg, "Broker-dealers and financial advisors: costs and payouts," Investopedia, February 12, 2023, https://www.investopedia.com/articles/personal-finance/062315/brokerdealers-offering-highest-payouts.asp.

14   Geoff Loftus, "If you're going through hell, keep going. Winston Churchill?," Forbes, May 9, 2012, https://www.forbes.com/sites/geoffloftus/2012/05/09/if-youre-going-through-hell-keep-going-winston-churchill/.